The education of the film-maker:
an international view

The education of the film-maker:

an international view

The Unesco Press, Paris
The American Film Institute, Washington, D.C.
1975

Ola Balogun shooting a scene for Nupe Masquerade, a documentary on Nigeria's traditional culture.

Published by The Unesco Press,
7 Place de Fontenoy, 75700 Paris,
and distributed in the United States by The American Film Institute,
John F. Kennedy Center for the Performing Arts,
Washington DC 20566
Printed by GEDIT, Tournai

ISBN 92-3-101262-2
French edition: 92-3-201262-6

Preface

This book presents a world view of trends, needs and potentials concerning the education of film and television directors, who are viewed as image-makers playing a central role in the present and future socio-cultural development of all societies.

The work is based on the papers and discussions of a meeting organized by Unesco on the education of the film-maker for tomorrow's cinema. The subjects dealt with included the following: cinema and television as instruments of culture in contemporary society; cinema as a major art form; the education of the film-maker as both artist and craftsman; ethical and legal considerations; technological and resulting social change influencing the education of the film-maker (videotape recording, cassettes and cartridges, videodiscs, cable antenna television, holography, satellites, miniaturized automated and inexpensive equipment, new distribution methods, experimental film movements, new audiences); programmes existing in different parts of the world for the education of the film-maker; current trends and new concepts in cinema education; new materials for film-television instruction; future directions; new curricula which are relevant to different cultural needs.

It should be noted that the chapters of this book cover the countries reported on in the papers written by some of the delegates attending this meeting.

Unesco is extremely grateful to the authors and experts who contributed to this meeting, and who are listed with their titles in the Appendix. The main points raised in the discussions are summarized in the introduction, which was prepared by Robert W. Wagner.

The views expressed are those of the speakers and authors concerned, and not necessarily those of Unesco.

Contents

Robert W. Wagner

Introduction

If we take the face of a clock as representing 3,000 years (or about the length of time man has been using systems of writing), the printing press would have been developed nine minutes ago; the telegraph and photograph three minutes ago; the telephone, rotary press, motion picture, automobile, aeroplane and radio two minutes ago. One minute ago the sound motion picture appeared. Television has appeared in the last ten seconds, the computer in the last five, communications satellites in the last single second, and the laser beam a fraction of a second ago.

The idea that film- and television-directors can be trained as such is not new. All the early film-makers, of course, began as amateurs (just as photographers had done almost a century earlier)—by trial-and-error and apprenticeship, often drawing upon what they had learned elsewhere—in theatre or painting, in science, in literature and architecture, and so on.

Film-making is costly. Film schools were established in certain countries, some with State support, others privately (often through or in universities). Many professionals who had solved at least some of the problems of the new medium through experience were inclined to say that you can't teach film-making (as others were saying that journalism, photography, broadcasting and other communication arts could not be taught). Nobody, of course, meant that they could not be learned. What the professional was really saying (often because he felt threatened by competition from younger persons who had the advantage of an organized intellectual and laboratory training) was that the gap between hard, practical experience and school training was too great to be bridged.

In many cases he was right. As various chapters in this book show, much of the early school training was over-theoretical, gave little practical experience, was in the hands of inexperienced teachers, and was handicapped by insufficient equipment and raw stock, so that the student had little real chance to learn. Film-making was learned instead by making news films on the streets, or else in the professional film studios. Prospective craftsmen and artisans (often organized in unions, guilds or other professional associations) learned from the fortunate few already engaged in this exciting profession. Many who were later to become film-makers learned the fundamentals and were moved by the possibilities of the medium by actually watching films in cinemas. Early films were also attracting visually impoverished and often illiterate peoples all over the world who were quickly learning to 'read' this new and visually as well as emotionally 'moving' picture.

The political, economic and cultural importance of providing formalized training for film-makers was recognized early in Europe, and only considerably later elsewhere.

A State school of cinema, established in Rome in 1935, was reorganized in 1948 as the Centro Sperimentale di Cinematografia, and came under the direction of Roberto Rossellini. A film faculty was established in the Academy of Arts in Prague in 1945. The Polish School of Cinema was instituted in Lodz in 1948, under the Ministry of Culture and Fine Arts. In 1947 the Spanish Ministry of Education established the Instituto de Investigaciones y Espériencias Cinematográficas in Madrid under the Ministry of Information and Tourism. As early as 1926 a German Film School had been established in Munich by Peter Ostermayr, which was later replaced by the Universum Film AG (UFA) Film Academy; recently film academies have been established in the German Democratic Republic, the Federal Republic of Germany and in Austria. Argentina, Australia, Canada, China, Egypt, Finland, Greece, Republic of Korea, and Romania among others are vigorously concerned with film education.

In North and South America, formal film education generally began in a small way in universities (Argentina, Brazil, Canada, Chile, Colombia, Mexico, United States, Uruguay). Sometimes it dealt with film theory and history, with little actual film production, and was seldom highly regarded by professors in the traditional disciplines.

In the United States, the university teaching of film presents a rich and variegated pattern, and usually reflects the intellectual and creative qualities of the university concerned. It is increasingly interdisciplinary, and its teachers must possess both academic qualifications and practical experience. University-produced films (student, staff, or joint productions) are shown to all kinds of audiences for all kinds of purposes, are produced in quantity (300–400 a year), and have considerable success in international festivals (Edinburgh, Vancouver, Venice and others).

This introduction attempts a synthesis of the papers submitted at the Unesco seminar in Belgrade in 1972 and its discussions there, covering four major topics: (a) cinema and television as instruments of culture in contemporary society and implications for the education of the film-maker; (b) cinema as a major art form and the education of the film-maker as artist; (c) technological and resulting social changes affecting the education of the film-maker; (d) current trends and new concepts in cinema education.

Cinema and television as instruments of culture

Vive la jeune muse cinéma. Car elle possède le mystère du rêve et permet de rendre l'irréalité réaliste. (Cocteau, 1939)

Film and videotape can be used for the private viewing of works of art and for private instruction or entertainment but film is essentially public, both in its making and normally in its showing. Both film and videotape can be reproduced almost indefinitely, and be seen by thousands or even millions. A film, like a child, takes on a life of its own, independent of its producer, and is sometimes used for an intent or purpose different from his. It may change with the time and place of showing; it may also be cut or altered at the behest of users or audience— and films both reflect and affect society.

In some parts of the world, children spend more hours watching television than studying in classrooms. People often base their judgements about current affairs on what they see on television. In some countries they may see television before they ever see an ordinary film, just as they may see a helicopter before they ever see a car or truck.

In India, for example, according to Satish Bahadur:

> The cinema, with a total capacity of 3.5 million seats, attracts an estimated daily attendance of 6 million—not much in relation to a population of 550 million, of whom over 70 per cent live in villages. Cinema has hardly

touched the vast majority of rural Indians, and is an almost entirely urban phenomenon.

It is estimated that at least half the world's population today has still never seen a film. At the same time, with the proliferation of image-making technology and distribution formats, it may reasonably be predicted that the applications of film and its influence on society will continue to increase. What was once considered as a toy has uses which range from the creative act of an artist to all kinds of political, economic, scientific, educational, research and therapeutic applications.

Film has changed journalism. The camera is a new typewriter. But it has been found that cameras can set events in motion in a way which was seldom or never done by the written word. The transition from a verbal to a visual culture is worldwide, even in places like India or the Middle East in which verbal and oral traditions are still strong. But satellites as a means of transmitting images are not equally available to all peoples.

Could equal accessibility be provided by the mass manufacture of inexpensive equipment for the production and reception of images and sound? Many countries have been unable to provide the television and film schools available to the larger nations, although democratization in this regard might stimulate creativity and a renaissance of their cultures.

The new audiences created by film have differing perceptions, needs and levels of visual literacy which complicate the task, and hence the education of the film-maker. New ethical and legal problems arise as it becomes easier to store, transfer, copy, edit and re-edit. Films beget films (compare old images used anew in Resnais' *Nuit et Brouillard*). Author's rights, copyright, and the personal element in creative works are frequently disregarded. In other arts, an artist will seldom appropriate the work of others and incorporate it in his own, and so risk destroying the integrity of both. Scruples of this kind seldom inhibit makers of experimental and some other kinds of film today. Many such problems were not foreseen in international copyright law, and one commonly held view is that, under the terms of the Berne Convention, any material may legitimately be copied and used for non-commercial, educational purposes.

Again, film and television sometimes deal in sound and pictures which involve invasions of privacy or even defamation of character.

Such issues must obviously be considered during the education of film-makers. The camera should remain a creative instrument and not an aggressive weapon; potentially, it is possibly the most humanizing force ever devised by man.

Cinema as a major art form

The Unesco meeting at Belgrade considered the artist in relation to the whole creative process, including the technology involved, and discussed the film-maker or director in terms which involved film, television and associated media.

It was generally agreed that creativity cannot be taught but that it can be fostered by the right type of learning environment, supported by the appropriate technological knowledge.

> . . . the attempt to develop 'artists' has been more destructive than constructive. We prefer to develop artisans. . . . To educate not the craftsman, but the creative artist—people who will be able to think, understand, and grasp the needs of their time and to meet those tasks in accordance with the time in which they live. . . . We must teach film artists, but also film message-makers—those who use film as a communication media and not only as art. We have two kinds of professionals—film artists and those who use film as a communication medium. . . . We believe film-making to be an art in the sense that painting, music and poetry are arts. But, like architecture, film-making is also a technique and a business; like the theatre it is entertainment; like literature it is a means of communication.

Clearly, the photographic-electronic image-making process is, like love, 'a many-splendoured thing' demanding a mastery of technologies and disciplines seldom required of the traditional artist. Two illuminating experiences were recounted at the meeting.

Mr Balogun said that his forefathers

> . . . did not value an object primarily because it was 'artistic' but because it fulfilled the function assigned to it, [and he recalled] . . . I was in a village in Nigeria making a film where I met an illiterate man who was also a fantastic musician, a builder, and recently a village gynaecologist. This set me wondering how schools can help direct creativity and stimulate young artists to be many things at the same time: to use the camera as only one aspect of their creative talents.

Mr Stevens related how Fellini, visiting the American Film Institute's centre, was asked by a student: 'Mr Fellini, we've seen all your films during the past week and we know you improvised. How do you do it?' Fellini replied: 'First, how I do it is that I'm a film-maker. That is my profession. But "improvise", no. For me, making a movie is a scientific process!'

Reviewing 'takes'.
[Photo: School of Communication and Arts
(Division of Cinema), University of São Paulo, Brazil.]

In the laboratory.
[Photo: School of Communication and Arts
(Division of Cinema), University of São Paulo, Brazil.]

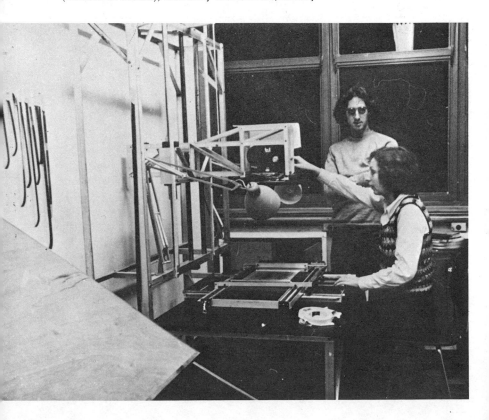

Hitchcock and others have said much the same thing. Intuition is not enough. In a technological society the artist must be in control of the technology.

Although automated equipment makes it possible for nearly anyone to make a picture, the professional film-maker must have mastered the basic theory and principles, the technology, the economic implications and, in addition, have an artist's eye and exceptional psychological sensibility. Like the Nigerian villager in the story, he must be able to do many things at the same time.

Perhaps the film-makers who most closely approximate to the traditional idea of an artist are cartoon-makers (McLaren to Trnka) or designers (Eames, Svboda, Thompson) who do both characters and background. Most film-making, however, is a collective effort in which the creator is involved at nearly every step with other people, including specialists in music, photography, dance, theatre and literature. A film is, by nature, interdisciplinary, and a 'film artist' is as elusive to pin down as Proteus.

As one speaker recalled, there have been three generations of film audiences: the fourth is a television generation. Television may be taking over the social functions of cinema, while cinema becomes more and more like the theatre, confined to a relatively limited number of viewers. This seems to be borne out by the proliferation of small specialized cinemas that are ousting the enormous cinemas of the 1930s in most countries; and by the generally high information content of television programmes.

Art is not the exclusive prerogative of dramatic, experimental and *avant-garde* films but can and should describe the quality of educational, documentary, scientific and other film forms as well. A well-photographed cross section of a biological specimen can undoubtedly have aesthetic quality. Some film schools train directors specifically for work in special sectors, and there is no reason why we should not also have great directors of great sociological, anthropological or biological films, for example. Some will become artist-educators in the sense that, as Jean Benoit-Levy once put it: 'To reach the mind the heart must be touched.'

The range and variety of films that can be made is being extended by advances in technology, and by the expansion of knowledge and of areas of human concern; film is no longer confined, either, to a linear, image-by-image sequence, but can make all sorts of combinations of moving and static, photographic and electronic images. There have been the kinetic studies of abstract movement—the early experiments of Léger and Richter; the classic studies in montage of Kuleshov, Eisenstein, Pudovkin, and Vorkapitch; and the more recent work of McLaren, Breer and others.

Underground film (including 8-mm and ¼-in portapack videotape) is a form that often seems to become fairly quickly acceptable to a wider audience—from which point onwards the maker often becomes more conventional. Pornographic films have their faithful audiences. 'Guerilla' films reflect a prominent feature of the present-day world. People who experiment with 8-mm film-making do not need to go through film schools. They make films which can be immediately discussed by the audience for whom they are made. This really represents the other end of the scale, from the increasing skill and knowledge required of the professional image-maker.

Technological and social change

Innovations affecting film technology include new developments in electronic and photographic image production, playback, and distribution systems; combinations referred to as mixed media or synaesthetic cinema; computer-generated images, holograms, audio-visual collages; 'living theatre' that utilizes motion pictures and stills, and so on.

There is a tendency to describe every innovation as 'revolutionary' although none seems to have rendered any preceding form wholly obsolete. No one has ever 'uninvented' anything. Contemporary photography, for example, has gone back in certain cases to the daguerreotype (invented in France in 1839). The revival of interest in radio is more than just nostalgia. The silent cinema is far from being relegated to the museum. The magic lantern and the lantern slide have had an astounding rebirth in 2×2 projectors incorporating zoom lens, automatic-focusing dissolve units, and automatically synchronized stereo sound.

The itinerant slide and film shows of the nineteenth century have their counterparts in the mobile units used today in many countries to serve outlying or isolated areas.

The mass media can convey images practically everywhere almost immediately, and at relatively low cost as the numbers of viewers increase, and thus constitute a potent means of promoting cultural and educational advance on a vast scale. Increasing miniaturization and automation means also that more and more people can actively contribute on the input side instead of being passive receivers at the other end.

These outlets for the amateur which provide thousands with a 'voice' could be therapeutic and creative in effect—even accepting George Bernard Shaw's caveat: 'The amateur photo-

grapher is like the cod who lays a million eggs to get one fish.'
Much modern equipment is specially designed for the non-
specialist amateur, being relatively cheap, simple to handle
with, in addition, a certain degree of interchangeability as between one medium and another. These developments obviously
affect the background to the education of the image-maker of
the future, and that of his potential audience.

8-mm film

Ordinary and super 8-mm film have enabled many aspiring
film-makers to experiment. Silent and sound (magnetic or optical) 8-mm films are now available in cassette form for use in
several types of cartridge-loading (although not necessarily
compatible) projection systems. It was hoped at one time that
the 8-mm revolution would provide the counterpart to the pa-
perback revolution in books, but this can hardly be said to have
happened.

Many film schools continue to use 16-mm and even 35-mm
film for teaching, but portable videotape systems are becoming
less expensive, and automated and miniaturized 8-mm cameras
are employed in many schools throughout the world. Students
are encouraged to use 8 mm for cinematic sketches, and 8-mm
film is widely used in ordinary school programmes. Richard
Leacock is investigating possible professional uses of super
8-mm sound-and-camera systems at the Massachusetts Institute
of Technology. With certain playback equipment, 8-mm film
can be seen on a standard television receiver, or be broadcast
on television. It is expected that all local television news in the
United States will be produced on super 8-mm colour film or
on $\frac{1}{4}$-in videotape in the near future. Prints are at present
produced from 35-mm or 16-mm originals by reduction printing. Blow-ups from super 8 mm to 16 mm may become as common as 35-mm prints made from 16-mm originals are today.

Videotape

Videotape recordings (VTR) now account for a large proportion
of television programmes throughout the world, and especially
educational and information broadcasts. Standards vary, but
2-in quad-tape is of very high quality and has been used in
producing programmes which may subsequently be transferred
to 35-mm or 16-mm film. Helical-scan tape does not use the
rotating recording heads used with quad-tape, but is wound in
the form of a long-pitched helix around a rotating capstan con-
taining the magnetic head. One full rotation equals a frame
suitable for colour or black-and-white recording and playback

Production still from the film, The Choice, *directed by Youssef Chahine (Egypt).*

from a machine of the same type. High-speed contact release printers are also being developed which will reduce print cost and increase volume on VTR copies. Portable cameras designed for amateur productions are available from several manufacturers in various parts of the world.

Videotape recording has been a very successful aid in teaching film directing, acting, camera work and editing.

Cassettes

Cassettes and cartridges are used to feed either raw stock or finished programmes into production or playback equipment without having to thread them into the mechanical parts. This facilitates loading, unloading, stocking and cataloguing, making the material as easy to find and handle as a book on a bookshelf.

Unfortunately, cassettes and cartridges used for tape, videotape and 8-mm film are not standardized and this tends to reduce interchangeability—including that of films and other teaching materials that could be used by film schools.

Videodiscs

Videodiscs, in their present form, are very much like standard microgroove gramophone records. They can be stamped or embossed on plastic material, scanned by a low-power helium-neon laser beam, and played back through a standard television receiver, either in black-and-white or colour. Each 12-in disc provides high resolution pictures for a minimum of 20 minutes and a maximum of 40 minutes playing time per side.

Videodiscs can be used to package all types of visual materials for mass distribution at relatively low cost. The playback unit (costing about $400) has an optical system using non-physical contact laser read-out (i.e. little wear and tear involved), can store approximately 40,000 million bits per 12-in disc, can 'freeze-frame' shots, affords random access to stored information, includes fast-forward wind and has a digital frame counter.

These various developments could be extremely helpful in film schools, in education, and in the home, but it is not yet proved that videodiscs and other new systems are economic possibilities for the average potential user.

Cable antenna television

Cable antenna television (CATV) is becoming a serious rival in some parts of the world to conventional television broadcasting. About a million homes are using it in the United Kingdom to

Production still from the film, The Land, *directed by* *Youssef Chahine (Egypt).*

receive a wide variety of programmes. It provides another potential outlet for the young film-maker.

Its great advantage is that it offers high-quality reception, free from noise and interference, and without an aerial. Television (and very high-frequency radio) signals travel in straight lines, and can be impeded by man-made or geographical obstacles. These are minimized by CATV systems, in which the viewing sets are connected to a master antenna either via coaxial cable or by microwave. The microwave system may prove more economic, and be able to reach more people in isolated areas. The system offers rich possibilities for continuing education in homes, offices, industry and farms. It could relay programmes, for example, to an interconnected group of study centres, training schools or universities.

Holography

Holography is a major innovation. It does not involve lenses, uses coherent light in the form of a laser beam, and produces a three-dimensional rather than a two-dimensional image. Holography (from the Greek, meaning 'the whole message') combines many technologies. Upon a photographic (silver halide) surface coherent light is focused through lasers. When the image is reproduced through the same coherent light system under optimum conditions, a perfect three-dimensional representation of the original is seen.

By miniaturizing the images so produced, it would be possible, for example, to condense the entire contents of the *Encyclopaedia Britannica* on a hologram measuring approximately 21 × 28 cm. Using lithium niobate crystals or chips, thousands of different images could be stored, and retrieved, one by one, by rotating the crystal in laser light. Such crystals (about the size of sugar cubes) may eventually permit the storage and playback of all kinds of images. These would be stable and almost indestructable, and could be played back in a variety of visual formats.

This 'information cube' could be used to store all the photographic, electronic, and printed information contained in a 50,000-volume library in the space of 1 cm, any part of which could be played back in less than a twenty-millionth of a second.

Satellites

The first live transatlantic telecast by satellite was relayed by *Telstar I* on 10 July 1962. In 1965, *Intelsat I* was put into orbit by the International Telecommunications Satellite Consortium, opening up a new era in international communications.

Television images constitute only a small portion of the load, satellites being mostly used for telephone, teletype and data transmission. They have immense potentialities for education, health and human welfare. Through multiple channels and controlled beaming, programmes can be addressed to specific groups of people. This has in fact been done in the Soviet Union, India and the United States.

However, satellites do open the way to the 'cultural invasion' of peoples and cultures lacking access to satellite facilities of their own; they should be entitled at any time to be able to turn such messages off as well as to turn them on.

Uniform international standards (compatibility, performance, operational safety) are needed. They exist for 35-mm and 16-mm film, but not for other audio-visual equipment, and the problems involved are difficult and immensely complex.

The International Organization for Standardization (ISO) and the International Electro-technical Commission (IEC) work through technical committees, subcommittees and working groups. There is also a Pan American Standards Commission. Unesco and the United Nations Co-ordinating Committee are endeavouring to secure standardization in communication matters.

The incorporation of desirable features (for example simplicity, quality, compatibility, compactness, efficiency, long life, agreeable appearance) into a single piece of equipment is often difficult, and might raise the price to a prohibitive level. The basic problem is to ensure the standardized international production of cheap and convenient audio-visual equipment, including standard and interchangeable cassettes.

However, it has been pointed out that the problems of putting moving images together for education or entertainment will be the same regardless of changes in technology; that new technical devices will not fundamentally change the way we teach film; and that we should distinguish between technological toys and useful additions to the palette of the creative artist.

Current trends and new concepts in cinema education

It is obvious that no single pattern of education will suffice to meet the needs of all learners. As a result of television and cinema, the learner himself is probably more visually sophisticated than he used to be.

The film-maker's studies have to be interdisciplinary, international and intercultural, but he should certainly also

Students at work in television studios.
[Photo: Hungarian Theatre and Film Academy, Budapest.]

Monitoring television programmes.
[Photo: Hungarian Theatre and Film Academy, Budapest.]

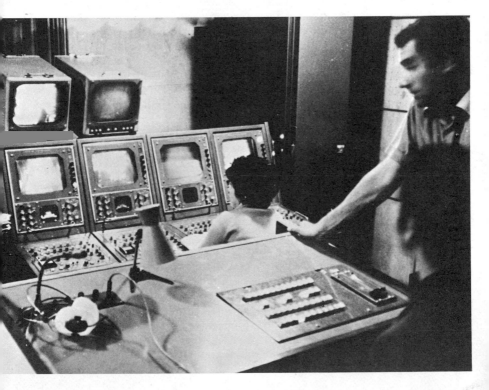

know his own culture and its needs. Students sent abroad to study should be chosen for their superior talent and their ability to enhance their training at home by the international experiences.

Future film teachers will include professional film-makers who will need to know more about both the learning and the teaching processes; teachers who will need to know more about both the learning and the teaching processes; and teachers who will need to know more about practical film-making. There is a great need for teaching materials: films and excerpts from them; film history on tape; filmographies; slides; videotapes; books; scripts in their original and post-production versions; production management records; set designs; memoirs. So far as possible, such materials should be freely exchanged, inside countries and internationally, together with student films, students, and film teachers.

The future will offer more ways to learn than ever existed before. The Open University in the United Kingdom is one innovation which may take many forms as teaching through film and television is extended to universities, institutes and schools.

More and more young people are seeking careers in cinema and television; they will need in-service adaptation or in some cases training for a new occupation. Knowledge accumulates fast: it has been estimated that by the time a child born today is 50 years old, knowledge will have increased over thirty times, and that 90 per cent of this knowledge will date from after his birth. Schooling will not end at a specific point or stage, and the education will depend largely on the skill, artistry, and wisdom and knowledge of film-makers.

A Goya drawing in the Prado in Madrid of a very old man hobbling along on two canes bears the legend: *Aun Aprendo* (I am still learning). Aldous Huxley once said that, in an age of heraldry, he would have chosen Goya's image as his crest and the words as his motto. The educational philosopher John Dewey defined education as the capacity for further education; the definition could be aptly extended to include film education.

Film and television students are working with students in other arts: a music conservatory, acting school, ballet school, collaborate with one of the best-equipped studios in Egypt, and with a school of architecture not very far away. Similar developments are reported from Belgrade, California and elsewhere. In universities, however, the film centre often seems to be too isolated from other activities, lacking contacts with the rest of the university and with similar centres outside.

Film students need to be able to experiment and learn

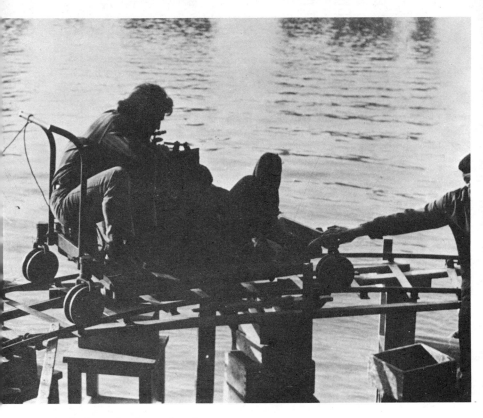

Students shooting on location.
[Photo: Hungarian Theatre and Film Academy, Budapest].

at their own rate, the teacher being primarily a consultant and adviser rather than primarily a source of information. This shift in student-teacher relations should improve teamwork and lessen any generation gap that may exist.

Under present conditions in Africa, balanced and comprehensive training can best be provided in a structure that is part of a university or closely related to one if courses of sufficiently high quality are to be provided at less than exorbitant cost. This of course does not mean that only those qualified to attend university should be admitted to film schools. The point is that, within a university, it would be easier to link the study of history, traditional culture, and the performing arts (dance and drama) with the apprenticeship of film techniques, practical exercises and exposure to outside influences. This would go a long way towards providing the prospective film-maker with a sound basis for practising his art.

Several Japanese universities have begun offering film courses, usually within their drama departments. Courses deal primarily with film theory, history, criticism, and writing, but some are beginning to make films. At several universities which have large numbers of painting, sculpture, and design students, film has been introduced into the curriculum, but not for the purpose of training future film-makers; the aim is to give the art student some experience of film-making as another of the various art media.

University education in the arts is often criticized for being over-academic and stunting creativity but there is an undoubted trend in universities all over the world to provide education for film-makers side by side with the more traditional institutes.

The great film classics constitute the basic 'literature' of film study. They should be made available to accredited schools and institutes on a low-cost, permanent-loan basis, subject to adequate safeguards to discourage pirating and unauthorized uses which at present operate to the detriment of both users and producers.

Film institutes should support the efforts of archivists to preserve rapidly deteriorating nitrate films. If these disappear, they take with them part of film history. The visual history of early television is almost non-existent, and unless a concerted effort is made to preserve programmes made on film, videotape or other media, students in the future will have only verbal and secondary printed material to study—the primary visual source will have vanished. Excerpts of films permit detailed analysis and comparisons, and provide illustrations of production problems or technical methods. Clearances from the owners are often difficult to obtain, as those who prepare educational material well know, especially in the case of works protected by copyright.

Despite the successful teaching use made of films, tapes, slide/tape combinations and organized learning programmes, no film schools or institutes seem to have specialized in producing the material in question. Combinations of books, films or film excerpts, tapes, slides, production books, videotapes and other materials could be packaged for use by film centres all over the world. Exchanges of filmographies, bibliographies, course descriptions and information about teaching methods and problems are desperately needed.

The twinning of film schools in different countries could be mutually rewarding. Exchanges between a school in an advanced country and a school in a developing country, for example, would give each an insight into the other's problems, and could lead, *inter alia*, to the production of teaching material that could be much more widely used than is at present feasible. Film teaching lags behind many other forms of education in this respect. There should be more experiment with new teaching methods. Film-makers could write about—and film—their work. Students could learn many technical processes on their own with the help of properly designed slide sets, films, diagrams and so on. They could learn from other students and, capitalizing on the difficulties they themselves have had to cope with, help to produce better basic textbooks.

International exchanges need to be as well organized as they are in science, through the scholarly compilation of information and its systematic distribution by means of publications, international organizations and conferences. The textbook concept could be widened to include cassette films, tapes and videotapes, slides and other media previously discussed.

The quality of teaching depends largely on the quality of the teachers. More amateurs are making films than ever before, and many of them teach in ordinary schools in the United States. And, like other studies, the language of film is best acquired young.

If it is true that those who can, do, those who can't, teach, the successful professional film-maker and television producer should be essential to film teaching—but he may not necessarily be a very good teacher: good teachers are as exceptional as good film-makers. This question needs careful consideration by film schools and university film faculties. Their programmes have to take account of the arts, the behavioural sciences, film, television, theatre, multiple-media, literature and photographic and electronic developments. They have to take account, too, of local conditions and resources rather than be devised by importing practices from abroad, but they should at the same time enjoy access to the best educational materials available from all over the world.

The role of the teacher is changing. He must now always necessarily be a learner also. Not so long ago, he could literally know all there was to be known about a given subject, had read all the books and articles, and might even be personally acquainted with all the experts. Today, it is virtually impossible for him to keep up with the periodical literature alone. Many students may well know more about certain aspects of a subject than their teachers. Teachers simply cannot afford to be presumptuous, or further widen the generation gap. Students have access to plenty of other sources of information and are no longer as dependent on teacher, classroom and school as they once were.

The extent to which ideas are changing may be illustrated by an example. In the Ivory Coast, it is expected that by 1980 all primary classes will be equipped for television teaching, and that 80 per cent of the children concerned will be taught through television—even though some of then may never have seen a cinema or even a photograph.

Such children will thus have an early experience of visual language as a 'mother tongue', and perhaps some experience later of 'writing with the camera'.

Future film education at higher levels will have to be much superior to that which is commonly offered in schools and universities today. Entrance requirements will be accordingly higher also, and the standards demanded before diplomas are awarded. Even today, some university programmes try to build on the student's previous academic work or experience— sometimes in apparently quite unrelated professions.

To make their film education more practical, students need outlets not only for their films, but also for scholarly work (for example history, theory, criticism); opportunities to help in arranging festivals, seminars and workshops; experience in film and television teaching and producing; and finally, better connexions with the commercial film industry.

The extent to which graduates can make films or are otherwise employed in films and television varies from country to country. Sometimes the number of admissions to film schools and, consequently, graduates are regulated by the anticipated needs. The Soviet institute described in this book has fifty to sixty directors graduating each year, specializing in feature, documentary, television, educational, scientific, or some other particular type of film. The institute has separate national workshops for students from Kazikstan, Georgia and other republics.

The Indian Film Institute regards film directors as creative artists who are at the same time aware of the social and cultural significance of their work. Students are trained, not in relation to some hypothetical distant future but to immediate film-making possibilities in India. The institute has good relations with the film industry; when students leave, they are pretty good technicians at least, and have little problem in finding a job.

Film graduates in Japan have recently not been entering the decreasing number of major film companies because of financial stringency in these companies and because they still insist on long apprenticeships which mean that, however qualified or talented, the newcomer must start at the bottom. The same is largely true in the United Kingdom, the United States and elsewhere, although a steadily increasing number of graduates are finding places in film production and other film sectors (cinema history, theory, criticism, teaching). The influence of such long-established centres as Paris and Lodz is unquestionable. Most young directors in Hungary are trained in the Béla Belaz studio. In the Soviet Union, 80 per cent of all those employed in film studios and film companies come from the film institute.

The influence of training centres is further extended by, for example, graduates who make low-budget, off-beat non-commercial films, and have a considerable role in making shorts, documentaries, newsreels, educational, children's and 16-mm television films. Their training is sufficiently diversified to allow this, and 16-mm films can be made with very little money, and distributed through, for example, universities. Over 200 companies in Japan produce some 1,000 industrial and 300 educational films a year. United States graduates find positions in the very large 16-mm industry; in local television and cable-television film; in teaching; in State and federal film units; and as small independent producers of short films for civic, non-profit organizations. The universities produce about 800 films a year.

Curricula

In both industrially developed and developing countries, curricula seem to be becoming more experimental and diversified. Each school has to keep in mind the needs of its local culture, but build upon certain common denominators, for example study of the great film classics; camera, editing and sound techniques; basic theory and principles. There must be flexibility in training programmes, for even though cinema and television will no doubt not change greatly for a long time, technology certainly will.

What of the future? Is the formal school, institute or training centre obsolete? Is society becoming 'deschooled'?

Unesco reports that a lot of the earth's inhabitants are still going full time to school: 400 million out of 3,500 million. National budgets for education are increasing in all countries. The same is probably true of film and television education, which can include many informal as well as formal types (for example the original 'spontaneous school' of cinema in Brazil, the 'documentary school' under John Grierson in the United Kingdom). So far as possible each country should offer a variety of possibilities to enable students to learn by working in association with teachers, and cinema and television professionals and actors. Their training should enable them to be versatile, and help to abolish any over-rigid distinction between the artist and the artisan. The good film-maker must be both.

The education of film-makers is too important to the future of civilization to be left to chance. Creative intelligence needs to be coupled with a sense of responsibility and ethical concern. This is becoming a major concern of governments, universities, schools and people, young and old alike, in a world increasingly influenced, shaped and mirrored by the films it makes and sees. Film offers a kind of universal mother tongue, constitutes a creative challenge that is rich in social promise.

As the Indian contribution to this book says so well: 'Film education, like any other kind of education, is an act of faith in the future.'

Ola Balogun

Africa

The development of film as an artistic medium probably represents one of the greatest achievements of our century, since it has placed at the disposal of the artist an unprecedented range of plastic and dynamic facilities, and potentialities that are virtually unlimited. Television, cassettes and various electronic devices provide vehicles that ensure to film an ever-increasing influence on communication between men.

The impact of film in Africa has been belated and is still limited. The reasons for this are not hard to find. Film is a child of the technological age, and industrially underdeveloped nations were obviously ill-equipped to benefit, having neither electricity nor a technical infrastructure. Films could not be shown, and so most parts of Africa remained outside their reach. Film is a highly technical art. Film-makers have to be familiar with sophisticated equipment. The high cost of film-making, the colonial subjection of African countries, and the absence of an indigenous audience to stimulate potential film-makers, explain why no African—except in the northern African States—had directed a feature film before 1960.

However, some urbanized Africans have been seeing films, even if only to a limited extent, for almost three decades. They were mostly popular films of the *Tarzan* and *Zorro* type, and they have had extraordinary success. Used to participating intensely in any public display, the African public found films irresistible. Actors like Edward G. Robinson, Errol Flynn and Tyrone Power become larger-than-life heroes. Even a film like *Saunders of the River*, with its exaggeratedly Hollywood-inspired image of Africa, has been so successful that Africans would swear that it exactly portrayed the Africa they know and live in. Though belated, the impact of film on Africa is thus considerable, and with more and more cinemas and television networks, there is little doubt that film will play a growing role in the lives of our people.

African background

Film has not come to a continent devoid of aesthetic traditions. Africa has had a long history of civilization, and art forms that have existed since the earliest times. Sculpture in wood, ivory, bronze, iron, and stone abound. The bronze heads of Benin and Ife in Nigeria, the Dogon carved masks and figures of Mali, the Mende of Sierra Leone, the Yoruba, Ekoi, and Ibibio of Nigeria, the Fand of the Cameroons, the Bakongo of the lower Congo basin, to mention only a few, have achieved world-wide recognition (perhaps the most convincing proof of this is the alarming numbers stolen or smuggled out of Africa every year to be sold to private collections and museums in the West). Other art forms include painting, architecture, music and dance.

Aesthetic traditions are thus well established, and artists have never been lacking. But as it is society as a whole that is paramount in traditional Africa, the individual artist was not glorified as in Europe, since his social function was the most important aspect of his work. Hence the myth that artistic creation is largely instinctive in the African artist, whose relative anonymity was interpreted as proof of non-specialization. Nothing could be further from the truth. On the contrary, the African artist is usually highly conscious of his means, and is eternally seeking solutions to his aesthetic problems. He is fully professional in the sense that he has generally had to undergo a long and thorough apprenticeship, and is usually as much artisan as artist, very skilled in making use of whatever material is to hand.

The idea that African art has degenerated as a result of contact with the West is also highly misleading. Societies evolve, and artists who imitate the past in order to preserve African culture 'pure' will necessarily produce the 'degenerate' art which shocks ethnologists. The latter have no one to blame but themselves. Would they ask contemporary Western artists to paint like Giotto? Where the artist is still living the traditional African life, his work will probably continue in the line of his forefathers, but where he has left it and is exposed to other influences, it is only right that he should strike out in new directions, even if he makes bad mistakes at first. Art is very vigorous in

Africa, and there is no doubt that the challenge of new art forms like film will be taken up by artists fully capable of mastering them.

African film-making

Film-making has its peculiarities, like any art form, and the would-be film-maker needs training (which can of course be acquired by direct experience) to master a highly technical and complex art. A man does not become a sculptor by picking up a chisel and hammer; he generally has to learn the technicalities from a practising sculptor before launching out on his own, although someone exceptionally gifted may forego this process. However, most artists need some form of apprenticeship. This is why art academies exist, and why film schools have been set up in some countries.

What form should the training of the would-be African film-maker take?

This article attempts an answer, with particular emphasis on the aesthetic and cultural aspects of such training, but recognizing also that too narrow an approach would not be very useful. Technique and art are closely interwoven in film: where does the purely technical end and art begin? It is not possible to examine cultural and aesthetic factors in film-making in complete isolation and we will, therefore, not attempt to do so here.

The African film-maker

No amount of formal training can substitute for artistic intuition and creative ability, but latent ability can undoubtedly be developed. How can this best be done in contemporary Africa?

Let us first consider how easy or difficult it may be for the African mind to cope with the mechanics of the film industry. The machines of the technological age are still relative newcomers in Africa, and therefore still to some extent objects of awe. People may need a minimum period of adaptation (extending in some cases over one or more generations) before reaching the stage of being fully at ease with them. Most rural Africans who lack a Western-type education are at first too baffled to be able to make a rational use of the resources of a machine; the persistence of a pretechnological mentality makes it too difficult for them. Indeed, one would not expect a rural European or Asian, in similar circumstances, to grasp the intricacies of film-making either.

While it is perhaps not absolutely essential for the film-maker to have much technical proficiency, an understanding, albeit instinctive, of the very complex and highly abstract process of transferring ideas into film is, on the other hand, an absolute necessity. Moreover, constant and prolonged film-going can be a most useful aspect of the film-maker's training, one from which the villager is normally shut off. Hence, the African film-maker will tend to be urban, to have become familiar with technology in one form or another, and to have received some measure of Western-type education. In consequence, he will probably be to some extent cut off from the traditional African cultural and sociological environment. This has obvious implications in considering his training.

Factors in training

Film schools must concentrate on the technical side, since this is the only really indispensable part of the training they can provide, but courses should also aim at broadening the student's mind and intellectual capacities; few acquire a formal education to university standard if they decide early to make a career in films, and film schools can to some extent fill the gap. It can be argued that, to be a success, an artist does not need a highly intellectualized training or much general culture, but none can deny that a broader education will at the very least always prove useful in the long run. Film schools in the Third World must also be careful to adapt the curriculum to the specific local needs.

What should a curriculum cover in the case of Africa?

The colonial experience has left the peoples of Africa with a deep yearning to recover their past and re-establish their cultures. This is a natural reaction to the situation in which most people found themselves after the colonial conquest, when an African was 'enlightened' only to the extent to which he was prepared to renounce his own culture and background in favour of the 'superior' culture of the foreigner. The desire to sweep away the effects of acculturation and rediscover the fundamental values of the African past has therefore become a vital aspect of modern Africa, and has had a marked influence on the content of its contemporary art. The potential film-maker should therefore be raised as fully as possible in the history and culture of his homeland.

If his background has in fact tended to cut him off from his traditional culture, his courses must help him re-establish contact and complete his education, for one who knows little or nothing of the culture and traditions of a people can scarcely

A still from Ola Balogun's Nupe Masquerade.

hope to make authentic films about them. The object of formal training should be to help him systematize and extend the useful knowledge he already possesses. With historical subjects, for instance, the film-maker has to have, or be able to acquire, a sufficient grasp of the costumes, language and behaviour of the period he seeks to portray. He may have advisers and experts to help, but just as he will get the credit if the film is a success, he will get the blame for any glaring mistakes that are allowed through. His grasp of the subject-matter must be comprehensive enough to enable him to supervise the work of collaborators and draw all the strings coherently together.

But although the curriculum of an African film school must include African history, traditions and culture, these are subjects that cannot be taught wholly in classrooms. Research on African history has been considerably expanded recently and, in comparison with oral sources, textbooks are still poor. Lectures can only provide a basis on which the student can build. The purely academic should be taboo. The student should be encouraged to undertake research on his own, not spoonfed with formal knowledge that will be of little use subsequently.

Any historical film obviously demands prior research by its author—just think of the amount Eisenstein must have put into the preparation of *Ivan the Terrible* or *Alexander Nevsky*. The task of an African film-maker might be even more complex, in view of the lack of written sources and the necessity of having to rely on oral tradition. While it is true that any person of average intelligence can piece material together from oral sources, it would nevertheless be well for the future film-maker to acquire as many as possible of the tricks of the trade while still a student. The course need not be too elaborate, since the object is not to make a pedant but to train him to think and organize his material.

The need for contact is even more pronounced, especially if the student has spent much time away from the traditional environment during his formative years, as is often the case in contemporary Africa. But whether or not he has remained in contact, training should help him to develop his powers of observation and his ability to utilize what he observes. This should be done as far as possible through field research courses and extensive travel in the countryside.

There should also be language courses, since most future African films will in all likelihood be made in the languages of our people. The film-maker should ideally be acquainted with several and, where possible, helped to acquire them.

Culture is a living thing, involving city executives, politicians and urban workers as well as a changing countryside. To observe, the student could seek employment as a factory hand, a dock labourer, or live a while with a peasant family as part of his training, using the experience as a basis for script-writing exercises, documentary reports or short fiction films.

However, cultural and historical training should not be limited to Africa alone, but also embrace other parts of the world.

Aesthetics

A film, to be attractive, demands the skilful and imaginative use of the resources of film as a language. A good subject will not in itself make a good film if poorly developed and inadequately filmed. The curriculum must therefore develop taste and the ability to devise treatment that suits the subject-matter.

However, one of the worst mistakes in film schools is the tendency to be unduly conventional in such training, i.e. trying to teach the student to make a film as Truffaut or John Ford would, rather than by encouraging him to strike out for himself. Not every film director can be a Mizoguchi or an Andrei Wadja, and while it is true that, unless the film-maker knows exactly what he is doing, complex aesthetic effects may obscure rather than clarify, there must still be adequate scope for discussion, experiment and exchanges on new forms and ideas in any film school worthy of the name.

As the aesthetic and the technical are interdependent, the best way of training in film aesthetics is to familiarize the student thoroughly with film techniques and photography, to let him see as many films as possible, and to encourage the discussion and analysis of films—but without pedantry. Courses in drama and the history of art should naturally be provided, as well as opportunities to experiment freely with montage and with new forms in film expression. Once the film-maker has become a professional, it is generally too late for him to experiment and develop his own theories of art. Film is a very expensive medium, and more often than not, the film-maker is greatly hampered by financial problems. The people who finance films do not like to risk their money on untried forms; denied the opportunity for trial-and-error experimentation, the film-maker is often tied to convention. The film school can offer virtually unlimited scope for experiment, and should allow as much as is financially feasible.

The tendency of some teachers in film schools to judge student films by unimaginative academic standards should definitely be discouraged. Often such teachers are not creative artists themselves. Perhaps greater care could be taken in selecting those who will lecture in film schools.

Relating training to traditional African art and art forms does not imply imitation, but rather the stimulation of intuition and talent by reference to the principles that contributed to the grandeur of African art in the past. This would also, incidentally, increase the student's awareness of the relativity of all aesthetic concepts of art. Our forefathers did not value an object primarily because it was 'artistic', but because it fulfilled the function assigned to it. The mask did not have to resemble a human face. In most cases it was a stylization, valued for its effectiveness as such, and its adequacy in relation to the purposes for which it was intended. There is much food for thought here for the film-maker tempted to seek the beautiful for its own sake in his films.

Teaching should concentrate on practical exercises rather than on lectures. The student should not only study the art forms of the past, but be encouraged to make documentaries that force him to observe them closely and well. Opportunities to familiarize himself with traditional drama forms and dance would certainly enhance his ability to turn such material to good account subsequently. He can learn a lot about the structure of narrative forms from epic recitations by *griots* and the stories of traditional story tellers. Man is basically the same everywhere, but differences in outlook and approach make for distinctive aesthetic patterns in different cultures; there is every reason to believe that attention to these factors in training film-makers would eventually result in the production of African films that authentically reflect the aesthetic and cultural backgrounds of our peoples.

The training must not be limited, however, to the African background alone. On the contrary, the student should be encouraged to study the art forms of other parts of the world, whether it be the Elizabethan theatre, Kabuki, or Kathakali, and his courses should give him as much knowledge as possible of art outside Africa. The benefit of comparative studies can never be sufficiently stressed.

Setting up film schools in Africa

The foregoing considerations indicate that particular care must be exercised in establishing the curricula and training programmes of film schools in Africa. Balanced and comprehensive training can best be provided in a structure that is part of a university or closely related to one if courses of sufficiently high quality are to be provided at less than exorbitant cost. This of course does not mean that only those qualified to attend university should be admitted to film schools. The point is that, within a university, it would be easier to link the study of history, traditional culture and the performing arts (dance and drama) with the apprenticeship of film techniques, practical exercises and exposure to outside influences. This would go a long way towards providing the prospective film-maker with a sound basis for practising his art. However, it must again be stressed that no amount of formal training will make up for a lack of flair and intuition, and that in any case training as conceived in a film school may in the end be in excess of the actual needs of the would-be film-maker. What cannot be denied, however, is that such training can develop talents that already exist and can give the film-maker a useful educational background that will enhance his chances of achieving his full artistic stature—justification enough, surely, for formal training of the type that can be provided in film schools.

Raymond Ravar

Belgium

Belgium became conscious of the importance of training film-
and television-directors, specialists and technicians towards the
end of the 1950s.

Belgian television began broadcasting, in French and
Dutch, late in 1953. A documentary school that had acquired
a lively reputation thanks to Henry Storck, Charles Dekeuke-
leire, Paul Haesaerts and a few others, was in decline.

There was no question of feature films or fiction, nothing
except swiftly quenched hopes, abortive projects, or plans
dropped as soon as they started.

Every effort ended in dejection, doomed almost automatically to failure from the start among the mass of other
obstinate, erratic efforts. The atmosphere was heavy, stifling,
failure seeming to attach itself fatally to this tiny country with
its two different cultures; for these various subjective and
objective reasons cultural projects remained singularly narrow
and timid, impotently realizing the objective truth that the only
production structures available were the faltering and soon
rigidly set arrangements provided by the new television administration bodies.

The diagnosis was simple: Belgium was suffering from an
acute constriction of its image and sound production and direction capacity.

People looked enviously at Sweden, and the sparkling
novelty of Ingmar Bergman's talent; or with nostalgia at Poland
where, its long martyrdom over, Wajda and several others were
offering an astonished world the hope-and-acid-glutted master-

pieces of its artists, all from the National School at Lodz. A few years later, Czechoslovak and Hungarian film-making was already more stimulating, less reminiscent of the impotence that invariably attached to every film-making project in Belgium. Meanwhile, the 'new wave' in France in 1958–59 had brought a ray of hope: the producer was not omnipotent, a film did not necessarily cost a million dollars—or even half-a-million.

Perhaps it was not a total dead-end; perhaps the right to express oneself in film could lose the bitter taste of never-ending disappointment.

Television—particularly Flemish—with all its faults, seemed at last to be dropping its exaggerated caution and timidity in production. Would it one day become a stimulator?

Finally, film and television schools were starting, too many of them it's true (Belgium also knows the multiplication of the loaves), but at least the battle against semi-amateurism had begun.

The ministries of culture, which were appearing for the first time among the political structures, concerned themselves, timidly at first and then more boldly, with the financing of film production. In short, on this square inch of bilingual territory, a new driving force appeared, far from perfect, sometimes felt to be amateurish or not professional enough. It was nevertheless a springboard from which new demands could be made by two generations which no longer felt themselves to be inevitable victims whose every effort must come to nothing.

These two generations found themselves caught up in the changes. At the first meeting of the year at the Higher National Institute for Theatre Art and Communication Techniques (INSAS) in November 1965, three fundamental questions were raised which it seemed then and still seems must be answered in the often cramped sociocultural and aesthetic context assigned (why?) to Belgium:

What is or would be the proper significance of any film, radio or television broadcast, play and so on whose audience would be automatically limited exclusively to Belgians?

Must our gifted young men and women automatically accept being uprooted (not to mention expatriation) if their standards of training and of expression are higher than those generally accepted in Belgium?

As international co-production becomes more and more common, must we automatically limit ourselves to contributing capital or equipment only?

An outline of a cultural policy began with the promotion of creativity in films and television; a fragile plant but free at last from the failure complex that had hitherto paralysed it.

That, in broad outline, was what happened in a small country in western Europe between 1955 and 1965.

An analysis will show why certain decisions were taken and will explain the elements, principles, and trends, socio-cultural and aesthetic, which implicitly or explicitly underlie them. Here the sociocultural seem the most important and irrevocably linked—like meaning to form—to their economic and political context.

Briefly, development (and renewal) were due to the following: (a) the evident need for producers and directors in radio and television; (b) Catholic uneasiness about the social role of the mass media (radio, television, press, film) and their effects on taste and minds, today and tomorrow; (c) a desire to understand more about audio-visual information in general (film and television language, the communication aspects of cinema, reception and perception of a television message) and the training of film-makers; (d) a determination to claim and win the right to express oneself in film, and gain access to the means of doing so with or without the help of the official television agencies, and also to get clear of the amateurism attached to every attempt at creative film-making or television.

Part (d) reflects deep cultural need, a strong and violent groundswell, the decision of two generations to break free from past frustrations. The sociocultural element in (a) is the demand by television producers for qualified personnel; in (b) the socio-political intention to influence society through the mass media; and in (c) getting people to think about the implications of the vast increase in audio-visual media, their relation to ordinary verbal communication, and the idea of at last providing creative training in film and television.

There is nothing unique in this, except that these links cross and recross in a particularly dense 'skein' on a tiny particle of land: 10 million people on 30,000 km², and speaking two languages.

Need for producers and directors

It was necessary to await television's fifth year and the stimulation of *Expo '58* (the world fair in Brussels) before a proper assessment was made of the need for directors and other specialized personnel. The parallel French-language and Dutch-language television services were born from radio, from which they recruited most of their staff; such staff still have an almost complete monopoly of producer jobs.

Scarcely any distinction is made between producing and programming. The two services offer an almost perfect example

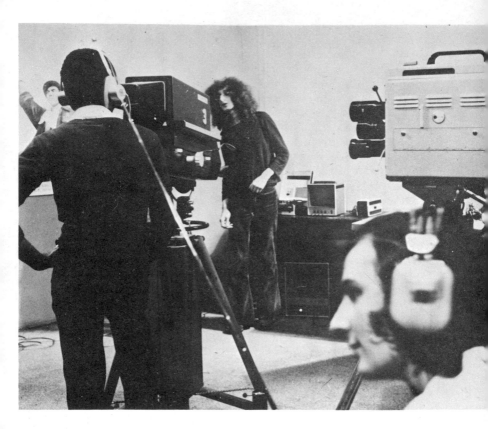

Student production. [Photo: INSAS, Brussels.]

The primary instruments in film-making.
[Photo: INSAS, Brussels.]

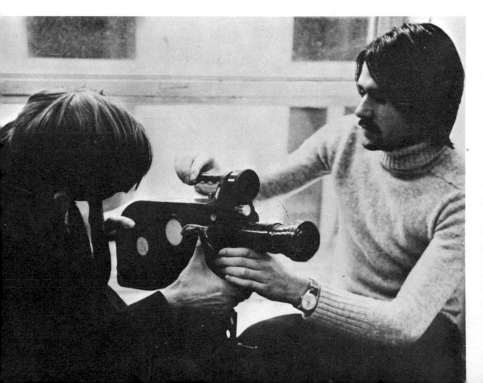

of the inextricable fusion of the two functions in the same person so brilliantly related by Pierre Schaeffer. He refers back to the way in which both production and distribution were managed in the film industry.

The first and second generations of producers/directors came naturally enough from the theatre, since a television play was considered to be more or less the same as one in a theatre. Men had to be found who could remain in control for the 30 minutes or the 90–120 minutes allowed for a play or programme.

Film directors (of whom Belgium had practically none) proceeded frame by frame—they could hardly do otherwise, working with a film industry that was scarcely even embryonic, and at a time when light equipment was not yet available.

They had to work with techniques so inflexible as to constitute a ready alibi for their short-comings—but this at the same time gave the television services a pretext for holding on to their privileges.

Flemish television did not escape the general rule, but was more ready from the beginning to give a chance to outsiders than the French-speaking service, which was obsessed with the idea of previous theatrical experience, and considered the model of French television—a pure product of Paris—sacrosanct; Flemish television tended to be influenced to a much greater extent by British and American models. It was also concerned with the deeper problems of finding a proper television language. It had no complexes about borrowing from radio and using live and living pictures. The 'theatrical' quality imitated from Paris continues to mark the other service.

However difficult it may be for the authorities to recognize the fact, it is hardly too much to say that Belgian television (especially French-speaking) had little trust in television, in the originality it could offer as a means of communication or as a new language. This was evident from the way it recruited producers (from radio) and directors (from the theatre).

People who did not fit into a category were suspect, as were also those who had acquired experience in longer-established (American or British) services abroad. 'Here, it's different . . .' (at the risk of being nothing at all), they were told.

The author and other 'rebels' in the French-speaking service realized what was wrong and saw that something else was needed. So did other staff and the growing television public. The desire to get away from amateurism, combined with the obvious need for producers and directors, alerted everyone in television, and from this resulted the schools.

Television producers now recruit their directors exclusively from among the graduates of the specialized schools run by the State or recognized by it. Independent producers and experienced directors are not however excluded.

A film or television background is not automatically demanded but to require it is becoming regular practice—to the benefit of all, including the public.

Young directors are attracted by the flexibility of electronic light-weight photography (VR 3000 camera), like some of their elders (Jean-Louis Colmant, Paul Roland) who look increasingly to London, Montreal or the United States rather than Paris.

Some of the teams who do in-depth reporting work flexibly, effectively and rapidly. Young graduates from the schools work with others trained on the job to furnish good if not outstanding reports on current events or retrospective documentaries.

These are up to international standards. Here Belgian (particularly French-speaking) television can happily disclaim any inferiority complex.

There can be no doubt that these major reporting programmes and documentaries, while varying in subject-matter from one country to another, from one television service to another, really are specifically creative. They faithfully—and with increasing sensitivity—reflect the societies or groups concerned and the underlying social reality.

Although concerned with facts, this television form is developing its own particular style, quite distinct from cinema varieties; it is taking over and assimilating all that is best in what is somewhat confusingly called straight cinema.

Associated with creative in-depth reporting are the television journalists trained on the job or in the universities of Brussels, Louvain and Ghent (which offer four-year degree courses in journalism and social communication). In conjunction with specialists in image and in sound, they form teams which report, analyse, criticize, take a hard look at current affairs, show what is behind them and how they affect social, economic and political life; on the aesthetic side they are constantly seeking new forms that may serve to heighten their efficacity.

This is something quite different from ideological films, whether fact or fiction, and from the engaged or didactic works of the Slon or Dziga-Vertov groups, Medvedkine and so on. They are made from within a system, not parallel to it, and broadcast. Their socio-economic originality lies in the vital questions they pose regarding political structures and options.

Seeing how it turned out. [Photo: INSAS, Brussels.]

The mass media and society

The Pontifical Decree of 4 December 1963 promulgated the Vatican Council Schema on 'the instruments of social communication'.

This governs Catholic thinking in regard to press, cinema, radio, television and their effects, i.e. the fact that, quite apart from individuals, they can reach the masses and society as a whole and act upon them.

Various prior encyclicals, including *Miranda Prorsus* (1957) and pontifical texts, discuss the mass media and film and television responsibilities.

Belgium is traditionally but open-mindedly Catholic. In Vatican council and synod discussions, the hierarchy has often opposed rigid clerical views; it freely organizes its own system of education which is mostly paid for, as a statutory obligation, by the State. Its teaching on the social purposes and Catholic attitudes to cinema, television, and radio is particularly well elaborated.

The degree in social communication and public relations of Louvain University and its research centre (CETEDI), the Flemish counterparts in the Katholieke Universiteit te Leuven, the Institute of Higher Studies in Social Communication at Ramegnies-Chin-lez-Tournai (a four-year course) are evidence of a Christian and Catholic desire to face these questions in a practical and pragmatic way, to train candidates for any job that may offer, or even contribute actively to their creation.

It was in this spirit that the Catholic Education Federation provided facilities in 1959 for the training of various specialists (including film, television, radio and theatre directors) in the new Communication Arts Institute (IAD) in Brussels.

Father Delepierre, S.J., defined the institute that year as an open Christian school which takes Christ and the Christian message as its reference value, where teaching is based on dialogue and on taking all points of view into account, and where the Christian idea is openly given full rein, particularly in matters of philosophy and the social sciences.

The institute is autonomous and is approved and financed by the State. Its programme includes the general supervision of the media of social communication and (in conjunction with the State institutes, INSAS and the Royal Technical Institute for Theatre and Cultural Diffusion (RITCS)) training specialists for television and film.

In view of what has just been said, it will not be found surprising that more training of radio and television people has been and is provided by the institute than by INSAS. This has been accentuated by the growing Catholic awareness, the development of television services (over 2 million sets for 10 million inhabitants) and new radio networks, since radio and television have a greater impact than cinema in and on society.

It was natural for the institute to devote prior—although not exclusive—attention to radio and television and to intermediary personnel who are neither directors nor journalists—less to creativity than to training people for jobs which existed or would be created in the Belgian Institute of Radio and Television Broadcasting (RTB).

This policy has been carried out realistically, as is shown by the number of RTB employees on the institute's teaching staff. Attention is also being given to the incorporation in new sociocultural movements of the solid traditions and experience of the Christian youth movements.

Preliminary research

The Catholic approach to mass communications just referred to is concerned mainly with social effects. A more sociological approach is adopted by the principal lay training and research school, that of the University of Brussels.

Professor Roger Clausse, who established the Institute of Journalism at this university set up a National Centre for Mass Media Techniques at the university's Institute of Sociology in 1957 which is still doing research on information, the message, the public, the sociology of television and radio audiences, mass culture, radio and television recordings, and so on.

The Institute of Sociology enabled the author to start early in 1959 on various fundamental and applied research projects on traditional university lines dealing with (a) economic and cultural structure of film and the film industry (production, distribution, exploitation) in Belgium in relation to the Common Market and the world generally; and (b) modes of perception of audio-visual messages and their effect on learning processes.

However, the most important part of the work done between 1959 and 1963 at the Film Seminar and the Experimental Centre for Cinema, Radio-Television and Theatre had no direct repercussions on the university itself, but led to the provision of a new type of teaching in a new institution, pioneered by our research at the Institute of Sociology.

Two trends underlay this development, both present (the second more than the first) in the teaching at INSAS. First, there was an attempt to start basic research on visual information, from a 'filmological' point of view (a term which disap-

First steps with the camera. [Photo: INSAS, Brussels.]

peared with Gilbert Cohen-Séat, its creator). The idea was pro-
phetic, but we still await someone to organize the multidisci-
plinary approach he had in mind. Second, creating was from
the outset the main problem for us, and in two respects.

Reference was made earlier to the violent desire to escape
from the impotence felt by aspiring film and television directors, and from the insufferably amateurish atmosphere and conditions of work.

Teaching film and television (theatre and radio also, but
that's another story) through seminars and study groups on
language, communication, signs, symbols, meaning build-up,
and so on, proved fruitful.

Experiments with a view to building up teaching methods
included criticism, theoretical lectures, debates, talks with directors and critics, practical reading and analysis at the editing
desk, production and direction of film and television sequences.

Initiated by a university research institute which designed,
organized and financed them, the Film Seminar and the Experimental Centre for Cinema, Radio-Television and Theatre led
finally to the creation of teaching possibilities—outside the
university. This shows how vigorous is academic resistance to
the admission of new trends or new disciplines, even when these
reflect social or cultural realities that are shaping a new era,
and a civilization in which the university itself forms part.

Thus, in any case, the initial professorial nucleus of INSAS
came into existence, with André Delvaux already playing a
decisive role.

The right to express oneself in film

As the right seems self-evident, we need say very little about it.
But rights are empty of meaning if the means to exercise them
are lacking.

A generation which can demand—and obtain—the right
to be taught creative techniques is better placed than its prede-
cessors, stronger, with more chances to succeed where they
have failed. That is the case today.

Still, the newcomers must not think that everything is
plain sailing because a school exists, and awards a diploma
which gives certain rights. Is a diploma in creativity imaginable?
. . . all this belongs to a future in which society and the graduate
are inextricably involved together.

A right to express oneself in film?

The formula has caught on, backed by the variety of
research experiments and attempts of all kinds outlined rather
than described in detail above; and it has given rise to an

impulse and a determination, a need to break free. The main contributing factors have been analysed, not so much historically as with the idea that a certain distance is needed to give perspective.

State support has increased, but payment is surrounded by red tape and fragmented—not at all what is needed in film production.

We now have ministries of culture which influence organization and exert no little pressure.

But, apart from the allocations for radio and television, culture's share of the national revenue does not reach even one per cent. The film aid selection committee deliberates, advises, but is not very adventurous. The radio and television bodies are poor and still more timid, greatly tempted to stick to programming and broadcasting and take the least possible risks in production.

The schools, finally, respond to needs and discern the main lines of future development perhaps better than any of the other institutions or agencies. They try to take advantage, to precede rather than follow, to foresee needs rather than deal with them mechanically.

Some new production groups from the schools are following the example of pioneers like André Delvaux and going more effectively and independently about using film as a means of expression in cinema and television.

Gérard Lenne

France

There is a great deal of confusion and uncertainty in France in regard to the training of the film-maker as a creative artist. Traditional ideas have been overbowled or simply dropped, new ones were produced by a variety of bodies which have taken up the issue, and a host of new experiments were developed to produce substitutes for outdated structures.

It consequently became almost impossible even to fix the outlines of a study because of the constant changes and the haziness of the two basic ideas in question: the very idea of educating people to become creative artists; and the socio-cultural and aesthetic content of film and of such education.

These ideas involve concepts which obviously cannot properly be analysed out of context, namely, cinema as a cultural and social phenomenon, and the way in which education in film-making is organized in present-day French society. As these contexts are not our purpose here, we need only allude to them; but as the problems in question are mostly only incidental to wider ones, the solutions envisaged must take on another dimension. In other words, it is practically impossible to be definitive; there is at present so much new theory and so many attempts to put it into practice that empiricism reigns unchallenged.

The questioning of institutions and educational programmes is certainly acerbated by the speed of change in the mass media, and the appearance of new audio-visual technologies which serve to show how ill-equipped the teaching structures are to cope with them. Stabilization is not for tomorrow. There must be a lot further trial and error, and the education of the film-maker in France is still in a state of flux.

Institutions and structures

The first question is whether such education needs specific institutions. It was—uneasily—agreed to need them in France up to 1967–68, but the film-making and television professionals did not officially recognize examination success as affording automatic access to jobs. The main training institutions were: the Louis Lumière National School of Photography and Cinema (Vaugirard) founded in 1926, which comes under the Ministry of Education; the Institute of Graduate Studies in Cinema (IDHEC) founded in 1943, at present under the Ministry of Cultural Affairs, the National Film Centre and the French State radio and television.

These alone can grant a diploma that is recognized by the profession. Because of limited vacancies, the attractions of film-making, and the advent of colour television and new channels, a rash of private schools (mostly short-lived) appeared before and after 1968. They tried to maintain a separate identity, but so nearly copied the aims and methods of the subsidized schools that they often looked like preparatory courses for them.

The existence of these private or semi-private schools and of rival official schools reflects the State's unwillingness to take direct charge of such education. Vaugirard admittedly comes under the Ministry of Education, but IDHEC is still governed by the 1901 enactment. The French State radio and television training centre is an internal part of a State agency. We still await the official unification of the existing establishments in a State graduate school on the lines of those which exist in Eastern Europe.

Institutions and structures become increasingly complex as cinema and audio-visual education in general try to cope with complementary tasks that are often difficult to tackle together: training the professional, and training the artist.

This study considers sociocultural and aesthetic aspects of cinema education in addition to the purely professional side, since our concept of education should be wide enough to take in all constitutions which the new structures may be able to make to it.

There is, for example, the increasing importance of the Saint-Cloud Audio-Visual Centre, and the work being done for quite some time on audio-visual techniques in teaching by the French Union of Organizations of Lay Education Through Image and Sound (UFOLEIS) and the National Institute of

Popular Education (INEP) at Marly. Audio-visual aids are also being increasingly used in film-language and film-history studies by the research and study units (UER), started in 1967 and 1968 in faculties of arts and humanities in the Paris-I, Paris-III, Paris-VII and (following the short-lived CEGA which attempted to compensate in 1967 and 1968 when the classes to prepare for the IDHEC entrance examination were abolished at the (Lycée Voltaire) in Paris-X universities, and in several provincial universities.

Two points may be noted: (a) film-makers are not always trained in institutes specially set up for the purpose; (b) people who follow courses at such institutes do not necessarily intend to become film-makers or television producers.

As these courses were diversified they in fact also began to attract students who were primarily interested in other audio-visual specializations, ethnological film-making, or a plethora of new promotional activities (cultural centres and so on).

Training the creative artist

Can creativity be learned? One common view is that the best way to learn cinema is to see films, hence the best school is the film library. Others reply that you have got to learn the trade. We are not specifically concerned with this here but realize that these questions cannot be separated and that the relevance of the technical-aesthetic issue which has led to so many misunderstandings must be considered.

Very different views are possible on this point, according to the importance attributed to personal gifts in the creative process. This factor cannot be completely eliminated and may even have a dominating importance in selection and recruitment when the vital question is whether or not the candidate is potentially an artist.

The official schools are modest in their claims. According to its constitution, IDHEC 'trains technicians who collaborate in creating'; the school at Vaugirard trains assistants for team leaders and states that creativity is not an end in itself at the school; the French State radio and television aims at the highest possible technological efficiency.

This is no minor point. It determines how the course will be planned. The curriculum, its division by subject-matter and the importance attached to each subject allow the candidate to know what will be required of him.

As we shall see, the trend now and during the next few years will probably be away from university-type testing which only goes to show that the candidate is proficient in a written

and spoken language, has a good background, and can express
himself in dissertation or discussion. Instead the purpose will
be to discover aptitudes which education can develop under
optimum conditions.

Specialized or many-sided?

The basic approach will decide how the curriculum will be
composed and constituted, and this explains both the variations
and the constants.

On the whole, the general trend is clearly away from specialization and in favour of variety. This is sensible, since film-
making itself is not split up into water-tight compartments.

As film-making has to be seen as a whole, it is illogical to
ask a candidate to choose his specialization beforehand. Whatever his eventual job, he will have to be able to follow it through
right to the appearance of the image on the screen. The Vaugirard school has always been against premature specialization,
and its courses form three general branches: photography,
sound and cinema. The accent is placed in each of these main
branches on mastering all the techniques involved and all the
instruments which it may subsequently be necessary to use.
The IDHEC programme was formerly varied in the first year
but thereafter quite rigidly specialized (for example direction,
production management, shooting, architecture and set design,
script-writing, editing). This is now changed. The candidate
has not to take a snap decision, but can make up his mind as
he gets the feel of the job.

It seems, in fact, that you shouldn't specialize if you want
to be creative in film-making since, to be really creative, you
need to touch on all the aspects.

The ideal in this sense is not simply versatility (which
would allow all students, even if not intending to take up the
same jobs, to follow the same course) but a really interdisciplinary approach within a changing educational system. Thus,
only the nature of the teaching is called in question. And it is
from this viewpoint that we shall consider the sociocultural side
which must derive from the education as a whole, and cannot
be the particular object of one or more subjects in the strict
academic sense of the term.

However well designed, no programme can guarantee to
teach creativity. Teaching which gives priority to awakening
creative desire and power and implicitly links art, culture and
social background is difficult to describe exhaustively and in
detail in a programme.

What are the programmes if not collections of subjects to

be studied in the usual classroom way? Traditional secondary and post-secondary subjects are taught side by side with new ones (for example film language and forms, film criticism, comparative literature, sociopsychology, history of art and cinema). But on the whole, the purpose is the same, whether entrusted to university lecturers or cinema professionals: a certain acquisition of knowledge.

Here we touch on a vital point, for this knowledge cannot really be acquired without practicals. The crux of the matter is the link between theory and practice, to which we shall return in discussing the forms and purposes of film education. As film education becomes a matter of working in teams after first working together in a group, the student is prepared to meet a new group—the film profession—and to appreciate its probable reactions, so that the theory-practice link has a vital importance to the social and cultural role of the film-making profession in society.

Irrelevance of the technical versus aesthetic dispute

But before considering the sociocultural aspects the mistaken idea that practice means nothing more than exercises to promote technical proficiency should be dropped. Once and for all, it must be understood that the technical and the aesthetic cannot be separated.

As aesthetics is too vague and subjective an idea for precise definition, we plead the inadequacy of 'technical' (as suggesting the immediately visible ability to handle instruments, equipment and so on) and substitute the term 'technology' (which suggests a scientific as well as a functional knowledge, knowing how to do something—as an executant—but also knowing what is happening).

Today it has become impossible to separate aesthetic arbitrarily from technological. The full picture must include sound, colour and movement which now entirely depend on mastering technologies which have been constantly improving for the last twenty years. A full grasp of sensitometry, for example, has become indispensable as film that is more and more sensitive comes on the market. Colour has completely changed the basic aesthetic working principles in television, showing clearly that aesthetics cannot be reduced to an abstraction, that it is part of the work and not simply an end-product or a gratuitous effect.

Traditional teaching, however (lectures on subjects forming a curriculum that was divided into a number of university-type disciplines), tended to isolate the aesthetic as something superior and unchanging; held to depend on personal taste and inspiration, it was ranged apart from technological studies.

The error is made all the more serious by the fact that technology continued to develop, and that accordingly, teaching based on such quasi-immutable principles does not consider itself obliged to keep pace with such development. It has become absurd, for example, to design a film set on models that were valid in 1946. The changes are mostly at the level of practical application; as the basic theory does not vary much, the theoretical part of the teaching is the most constant. But aesthetics is not really separable from the laws of physics, from either accoustics or optics. Cinema (or television) exists as an art in its own right as well as demanding a unique range of qualities and knowledge in its creators.

As these qualities and this knowledge are obviously not inborn, the major educational problem is how best to acquire them, and this involves finding the proper balance between theory and practice.

This works both ways, i.e. it is just as necessary to get away from the idea of an exclusively theoretical or even book knowledge ('What is really asked for . . . is a theoretical and hence book knowledge of cinema history'—this phrase is taken from the IDHEC admission conditions and syllabus for 1965 and relates to giving an equal chance to all candidates, but it is nevertheless disquieting) as from the idea of keeping the distinction between theory and practice and taking practice simply to mean putting into practice once the theory has been learned. This would place too much emphasis on the material means which are undoubtedly essential but should not be made to serve as an alibi for short-comings in the education.

The theory-practice link-up must be a living part of any truly effective education. It necessitates an educational policy which does not limit itself to perfecting of technological learning processes—unless the purpose is merely to supply the cinema and its advertising fringes with good technicians who can do perfectly well any job that is given to them. In that case, care has to be taken of the growing aesthetic requirements demanded in such employments, but this does not adequately care for the sociocultural aspects of film-making, aspects which are then left to look after themselves.

The most important and urgent question would therefore seem to be: How can film education be best organized with due regard to the social and cultural role of the film-maker in society?

Social and cultural aspects
of the film-maker's education

The prospective film-maker has to confront a culture and a society. How will he react, how use his newly acquired technical qualifications to find himself?

There can be no question of imposing or prescribing attitudes. Existing schools have done little positive to help beyond including a subject in the syllabus—social psychology—which, at best, can only be a popularization. Once again, in other words, we have a book exercise which might help in making certain choices, but can hardly do more than give a spectator's inkling of the social world.

New ideas being tried out (particularly at IDHEC, which is changing all the time) include trying to find by experiment an original and sensible working method for each student to replace the old division into a course and practicals (which often went to ridiculous lengths in making a distinction between the two); groups would work under tutors on both outside and laboratory tasks, more or less independently, subject only to constructive criticism of what they are doing.

It is not the end-product which is the subject of criticism and self-criticism, but the work in hand. This transforms teaching into real research. The students do not know their programme in advance, but discover how to express themselves by actually trying to do so. The method may involve mistakes, but even error can be helpful. This continuous research prevents fossilization; the tutors guide and encourage initiative in the student instead of telling him what to do in the manner of the former professors.

These film-makers or television producers are building a culture, and must face up to the implications. Their view of their role should not be bookish, but be firmly based on contact with reality.

What forms should this most important contact take? The IDHEC preliminary entrance test in 1971, for example, required the candidate to compile a dossier on a study carried out over several months on a subject of his choice (a person, couple, social group, occupation or place) consisting of documents (newspaper articles, pamphlets, brochures, reports of discussions or interviews, books, and so on) and thirty photographs (taken by him or acquired) which illustrate, comment or explain. This kind of exercise is clearly a type of lived-out experience which can be told and transmitted in audio-visual terms.

This may look like a piece of reporting—but that requires

the same kind of approach as writing a scenario: both involve imagination.

The other qualities demanded (formerly cultivated by written and oral exercises) are skill in selecting (personally or as demanded) and ordering material. From a series of given sounds (real or artificial), for example, can the student select and organize a sequence which directly indicates or reveals musical sensitivity, and has its own logic, dynamics and original significance?

The education of a film-maker can be greatly facilitated in this respect by television equipment, which provides immediate awareness of audio-visual duration, organization and composition, and of relations between image and sound. Here the generalized use of videotapes and videocassettes could be decisive.

A certain dated concept of film-making education, involving traditional university education and lectures as a preliminary, seems definitely dead. Current teaching follows two lines: high-level professional and technological training aiming at maximum efficiency; or the continuous investigation of various audio-visual possibilities with the aim of encouraging originality. Each has its place, and they are both finally complementary.

In either case, technical progress and the ever-widening use of audio-visual methods constitute both the major problem and the best prospect. Teaching must keep pace with rapid change and new inventions (super 8, videocassettes, videotape recorders, slides, and so on) that are in increasing use (teaching, amateur, underground, political films). The aims of a school are no longer confined simply to providing professional education for prospective film-makers, and the alternative to being open-minded is sclerosis. A veritable mutation is taking place.

Satish Bahadur

India

Cinema came to India in 1896 almost immediately after its invention in the West, and was introduced among a traditional, rural and predominantly illiterate population. The first Indian film, D. G. Phalke's *Raja Harishchandra* (1912) nevertheless showed that this society could adapt an imported technology to its purposes. Sound technology arrived in 1930. By the mid-1950s India was the world's second or third largest producer, making films in Indian languages for growing audiences, using its own characteristic conventions (use of song and dance, theatricality in scenario treatment, acting and dialogue), but showing little consciousness of the specific possibilities of film language. Indian cinema was hardly at all affected by creative developments in the international art of the film, both film-makers and mass audiences being isolated in a self-contained, closed world.

Some factors of change became perceptible after independence in 1947. A turning-point was reached in 1955 with Satyajit Ray's *Pather Panchali* (Song of the Road). Ray was self-trained. Working completely outside the established Indian conventions, he produced a film which was a great work of art and a remarkably true reflection of Indian life. This film gave rise to a new consciousness of the possibilities of film language and the artistic and social roles of cinema in Indian society. Other film-makers have since produced artistically significant films which ignore the conventions and commercial patterns, and various groups are working to improve quality: film societies, the Film Finance Corporation, the International Film

Festival of India, the Film Institute of India and the National Film Archive of India. The new consciousness is still confined to a minority, but it is offering a vigorous challenge to the commercial attitude of the film industry, and it produced perceptible results during the 1960s. This is the background to the ideas and programmes for the training of film-makers.

Phalke

Cinema meets a need for mass entertainment in an expanding, post-literacy, industrial society. It spread quickly over the Western world, and in further search of paying audiences, came to India as well. The Lumière programme was shown in Bombay in July 1896, seven months after its world *première* in Paris. Primitive cinemas sprang up in India to show films from Denmark, France, Germany, Great Britain, Italy and the United States.

But this marvel of the moving pictures recounted alien stories only. Why not put Indian stories on Indian screens? D. G. Phalke was interested in theatre, painting and magic as well as being familiar with the technologies of photography and printing. He soon unravelled the mysteries of the new medium. With imported equipment and raw stock, he produced the four-reel *Raja Harishchandra* (King Harishchandra) in 1912— the first Indian film.

Phalke regarded cinema as a popular art. Films should tell stories recognizable by the largest possible number of Indians. This requirement was answered by popular variants of mythological tales. The new visual medium could use trick effects to bring to life on the screen spectacular, magical and miraculous elements from the popular religious imagination, and did so in *Raja Harishchandra*. Mythological films became the dominant genre. *Raja Harishchandra* was influenced by another popular art, the oleographs of Raja Ravi Varma, who died in 1906. He depicted Hindu gods and goddesses in the most sentimental style of Victorian painting, and cheap colour reproductions of them were extremely popular.

Phalke's first and subsequent films were rudimentary narrative in form, front photographed, and the acting, make-up and costumes were derived from the Indian folk theatre.

Regarding cinema as a popular art, Phalke drew upon other popular arts, but not from the Indian classical heritage, for example the cheap oleograph and not Ajanta frescoes or Mughal and Rajput paintings; the crude elements of folk, and not the glories of classical Sanskrit theatre; not the underlying spiritual concepts of the Indian religious epics (the *Ramayana* and the *Mahabharata*) but their most obvious ritualistic and superficial elements and the magical and the spectacular exploits of Hindu gods and goddesses. For films which would assimilate and portray the deeper values of Indian life and culture, India had to await the work of Satyajit Ray, four decades later.

Popular cinema

The introduction of sound provided an assured home market, and the four decades since 1931 have seen the Indian film become unique as a form of popular entertainment among the urban masses. Dialogues in Indian languages ensured easy understanding of the plot. Songs and dances were added entertainments in the simple stories of romance, adventure and melodrama (Indian or Hollywood). There were no parallel developments in serious music, dance, theatre or television (still embryonic in India). The 35-mm feature film industry makes 400 films every year (in Hindi and eleven other regional languages). These are shown in 4,500 permanent cinemas, while 1,800 touring cinemas take films to small towns and to the countryside. The cinemas with a total capacity of 3.5 million seats attract an estimated daily attendance of 6 million—not much in relation to a population of 550 million, of whom over 70 per cent live in villages. Cinema has hardly touched the vast majority of rural Indians, and is an almost entirely urban phenomenon.

Earlier socially conscious films

Popular films account for possibly 95 per cent of the annual production. However, there have also been films seriously concerned with contemporary problems. The lead was given in the 1930s by V. Shantaram of the Prabhat Film Company, P. C. Barua and Debaki Bose of the New Theatres, and Himansu Rai of Bombay Talkies, who dealt with social reform in films of human and patriotic interest. During the 1930s and 1940s, there were Nitin Bose, Chandulal Shah, K. Subrhamanyam, Mehboob Kahn, B. N. Reddi, Vijay Bhat, Sohrab Modi, Master Vinayak and Gajanan Jagirdar; and from the 1950s onwards, Bimal Roy, K. A. Abbas, Chetan Anand, B. R. Chopra, Raj Kapoor, Guru Dutt, Mohan Sehgal, Hrishikesh Mukherjee, Sunil Dutt, Manoj Kumar, D. Jayakantan and Ramu Kariat and others.

The history of cinema, like any other form of history, is not static, a statement of facts accepted once and for all. Every generation applies contemporary analytical norms to older valua-

Students shooting exteriors in a village location.
[Photo: Film and Television Institute of India.]

Shooting in a forest glade for the student production
Vilaap *(The Lament) which won the Golden Ibex Award*
at the Teheran Film Festival.
[Photo: Film and Television Institute of India.]

tions and seeks fresh material from earlier periods. The decade of the 1960s has been crucial for Indian cinema in two respects. First, there is now a heightened understanding of the artistic and social values of cinema thanks to the quantity of films and critical books and journals available, and to experience in teaching cinema. Second, earlier Indian films can be submitted to critical study at the National Film Archive of India, which was set up as a part of the Film Institute in 1961 and became autonomous in 1964. These two developments have made it possible to evaluate the tradition of film-making in India.

During the 1960s, the trend was progressive. Satyajit Ray continued to make films. Mrinal Sen and Rikwik Ghatak had started about the same time as Ray and shared his views. Their films were received with interest. Tapan Sinha in Calcutta and Hrishikesh Mukerji and Basu Bhattacharya in Bombay, though working in the commercial cinema, produced good films which also had a social content. The Film Finance Corporation, after a halting start, embarked on a bold programme of financing low-budget off-beat films that has allowed a new set of film-makers to make their first feature films (Mani Kaul, Basu Chatterjee, Kantilal Rathod, S. Sukhdev, Satyadev Dubey, Shivendra Sinha, Prem Kapoor, Arun Kaul, Chidaranda Dasgupta, Raj Marbros, Adoor Gopalakrishnan and Kumar Shahani). They are using fresh themes, and ignoring commercial studio conventions. Their backgrounds are varied (Film Institute, film societies, short film-making). Even the commercial cinema is now making low-budget films with new kinds of stories and new actors and actresses. Artists and technicians trained at the Film Institute are taking an active part in these new developments.

During the 1960s the number of film societies in the cities increased to about 200, with an estimated membership of 40,000. Films for festivals and special programmes were obtained by embassies, film societies and the National Film Archive. Writing on cinema has become more sharply critical. More space is being given to the progressive film, even in the popular film journals, and in the daily press, in English and in Indian languages. There is a proposal to start art cinemas for off-beat films which cannot afford commercial cinema costs. Following a number of serious breakdowns in the film industry, there is now a move to set up a 'film council' to regulate its internal workings. The problems of censorship were investigated by a high-powered committee, appointed by the government, which has made important recommendations to tone up the quality of commercial films.

The education of the film-maker

A plea for an institution to teach film-making in India was made by D. G. Phalke, the first Indian film-maker before the Indian Cinematograph Inquiry Committee in 1927, but the idea was premature. Until 1961, the film industry depended entirely on an apprenticeship system in the studios for both actors and technicians (Bombay Talkies in Bombay, the New Theatres in Calcutta and the Prabhat Film Company in Poona). A recommendation by the 1951 Film Inquiry Committee to establish a national film institute was not followed up at the time. The appearance of *Pather Panchali* in 1955 had a profound effect, and the Film Institute of India was eventually established in Poona by the Government of India in 1961.

Madras and Bangalore institutes

Training is now also available in the Institute of Film Technology, Madras, and the Jayachamaraja Polytechnic, Bangalore. The Madras institute offers courses in film laboratory techniques, cinematography and sound recording, with the emphasis on technology rather than on the creative side. The scope was somewhat widened recently by the introduction of elementary courses in film appreciation, history of cinema and Indian culture. The Bangalore polytechnic gives purely technical courses in cinematography and sound recording.

Poona institute

The Film Institute of India, Poona, as a professional film school, is concerned with the creative and aesthetic aspects of the education of film-makers. It offers three-year courses leading to diplomas in film direction, script-writing, motion-picture photography, and sound recording and sound engineering; and two-year courses in film-editing and film-acting. Since 1971, the range of courses has been enlarged to include television training, and the name of the institute has been changed accordingly to the Film and Television Institute of India. Since Poona has no television studio, the television section of the institute was temporarily housed at the Delhi Television Centre, where an in-service course was organized for people already employed in broadcasting and telecasting. A grant of over $1 million from the United Nations Development Programme (UNDP) Special

Fund is being used to obtain equipment, experts and related services, and the buildings are under construction at Poona. The entire plan is being carried out by UNDP experts with Indian counterparts.

The film section of the Poona institute has now been ten years in existence. It admits ten to twelve students yearly to each course on the basis of tests and interviews. Students come from all over India and from Asian and African countries.

Facilities

The institute is housed in its own twenty-one-acre campus at Poona which includes an outdoor forest lot. It has film-making and teaching facilities, and 35-mm and 16-mm camera, editing, sound and laboratory equipment, projection theatres and class-rooms. A regular staff of thirty teachers deal with the various specialities, namely direction, script-writing, cinematography, editing, sound recording and sound engineering, acting, appreciation, production, art direction, music and dance. Eminent outsiders are frequently invited to teach and to assist in academic matters (selection of students, drafting of courses, examinations). The library has 10,500 volumes on cinema and the other arts, and receives most of the important film magazines from all over the world. The institute has its own film library of international and Indian classics for teaching purposes. The National Film Archive of India, which is also housed at the institute, gives instant access to a very wide range of films.

International contacts

The Film Institute has always stressed the importance of the international aspect in the training of the film-maker, and avoided the cultural isolation which had previously been a limiting factor in the Indian cinema. The initial teaching plans were drawn up in consultation with Rémy Tessonneau and drew upon French experience. Jagat Murari, principal of the institute, visited Moscow to study methods there. Jerzy Toeplitz, then rector of the Polish Film School, came to Poona for an extended stay. The teaching programmes from other film schools and from universities in the United States and Japan were constantly consulted, and membership of the Centre International de Liaison des Écoles de Cinéma et de Télévision (CILECT) enabled the institute to keep in touch with film teaching in other parts of the world. The British Film Institute provided copies of international film classics. The institute received teachers from France, Poland, the Soviet Union, and the United Kingdom for long periods, and film-makers and scholars from all

The editing room of the Film Institute of India.
[Photo: Film and Television Institute of India.]

parts of the world have given talks. Two short courses for short film script-writers from Asian countries were organized in collaboration with Unesco.

Approach

The institute has firmly avoided a narrowly technical approach in its courses. As film-makers are creative artists who have to use technology as a basic element in their work, technical studies must be a fundamental part of their training, but this must be given against a general background which enables them to appreciate the aesthetic and social significance of the film as art. The next two sections explain how this is done.

Orientation courses

During his first months at the institute, every student, irrespective of specialization, takes orientation courses which relate film-making to a larger framework, and cover the basic principles of film direction, photography, editing, cinematography, sound recording, production economics, acting, film history, art direction and design.

Background of film culture

The screening of a wide range of international and Indian films provides a background to the academic activities. Apart from films related to specific parts of the programme, evening shows arranged by the institute or the National Film Archive can easily be attended by students, most of whom live in institute hostels or in other accommodation near by. Very animated discussions among students and with the teachers often follow. It is hard to define in formal curriculum terms the value of a lively critical atmosphere which is created by impromptu discussions outside the classrooms, but its educational value is indisputable.

Poona has no art cinemas; indeed no Indian city has any. Its commercial cinemas show popular Indian and a few American films only. Students of a film institute in a European or American city could presumably see a wide range of films in local cinemas, but not in Poona. Hence the institute has to provide this additional service as well.

Film direction course

Initially a two-year course combined script-writing and direction practice, after which a student could, if he desired, specialize for one year in film direction. Since 1966 there has been a three-year course in film direction. Its objectives were stated as follows in 1969:

Inculcation of the film sense by thorough grounding in the film language and an accurate knowledge of all branches of film-making, leading to inventiveness and ability to create in the film medium.

Improving the quality of the student's mind in relation to the total Indian environment, leading to ability to think deeply, arrive at considered opinion and to be able to comment and interpret. This would involve development of the awareness of Indian life and society through observation and actual experience in depth, built up on the background of culture, psychology, sociology and the study of other arts.

A thorough understanding of the human and technical problems of a film-making unit necessary for the successful leadership of a film unit.

A full understanding of the technologies involved in film-making and knowledge of what the members of the unit working with their equipment can do and cannot do.

The immediate objective of finding a place in film-making in India.

It will be seen from the above that the institute views a film director as a creative artist who is also aware of the social and cultural significance of his work. This ensures that students are being trained to work, not in some hypothetical distant future, but within immediate film-making possibilities in India. These possibilities have been growing considerably in recent years. The institute's good relations with the film industry have helped in finding openings for students, who find jobs making popular films on the fixed studio pattern and low-budget off-beat films. There is a big and growing demand for shorts, documentaries, newsreels, educational and instructional films, children's films and 16-mm television films. Former students are engaged in making all of these kinds of films. The training programme for directors is sufficiently diversified to allow this and reduce dependence on studio-made entertainment films as a way of making a living.

All students of the director's course are university graduates. The course lasts three years of two terms each: 1 July to 15 October (12 weeks), and 15 November to 30 April (18 weeks).

The future

The film director course is bold in concept and practice. Difficult to design, it is by no means easy to execute, and is constantly being modified as experience accumulates. It is also bold in relation to the Indian film background against which it was planned. For several years there were doubts in the film industry about the viability of the institute itself and of its programmes. But its graduates have continued to find suitable positions in the various sectors of film-making in India, and there is now a mild appreciation of the institute and what it is trying to do.

The institute is of course just one element in the Indian film situation, and part of the minority who are struggling to improve upon the well-established traditional standards and values of the commercial film. What happens at the institute has an influence on the film industry, and vice versa. Its universal approach to film teaching is often misunderstood; students are accused of being un-Indian in outlook (whatever that might mean). But all this is normal in any situation in which new ideas are contending with older values.

Cinema still has a lowly place in the cultural life of India, and the institute does not always attract the best of our young people for training. Many students are misled by the false glamour of cinema and ideas derived from their experience of commercial films. Attitudes may change under the cultural influence of the institute, but not always. In many cases the commercial attitudes persist: students acquire a great deal of technique, but not necessarily the deeper values. Even in such cases, however, it is reasonable to hope that their training at the institute will help eventually to improve the quality of entertainment films. A minority develop a profound aesthetic sensibility and consciousness of social values. Their first films may be worth waiting for. An institute can, at best, attempt to impart technique, and promote a certain sense of values. It can help a student to learn, but not ensure that he actually does learn, much less predict how he is going to shape up in the future.

Film education, like any other kind of education, is an act of faith in the future. In the last twenty years, many economic, social and cultural agencies have been set up in India on the basic premise that they will generate new ideas to replace those which have become antiquated and stratified. The campaign for modern agriculture or more steel or improved health is a struggle for a better India; so also is the effort to build a more purposeful and artistic cinema. The Film Institute is attempting to make its small but vital contribution, and its very existence is another act of faith in the future.

Naosuke Togawa

Japan

Film in Japan, during its earliest days, derived largely from
Kabuki and the traditional theatre. But film did not for long
continue to be merely 'canned theatre'. Film-makers soon realized that film was a different art, and began to try out various
technical experiments. Talented pioneers developed their creative skills, and these early trials in turn stimulated others.

One of the leading Japanese directors of the silent-film
era, Daisuke Ito, who made *tidai geki* (period dramas), tried
a startling technique to convey the bloodiness of a samurai
sword blow. Between the shot of the blow being delivered and
one of the victims being wounded, he inserted two or three
frames of pure red film, but in that filmic moment, the audience
felt strongly the sudden gush of blood. In such ways, by trial
and error, the early film-makers developed new techniques.

The next generation also had to resort to trial-and-error
methods, but profited from the experience of their predeces-
sors, since film production was also a form of organized education in film techniques. Directors taught their assistants while
actually producing films; a director guided the work of assistant
directors, and they collaborated with him in script-writing. But
assistant directors worked hard, were not well paid, and no
matter how much talent they had, were obliged to wait their
turn (for a chance to direct) more or less according to the order
in which they had entered the studio. This apprentice-type
situation was the same for prospective cameramen, and it continued for a long time.

During the early days of sound film, companies provided

training schools for film-makers in their own studios. The most urgent need was for script-writers. Producers had originally depended on novelists or journalists, but as the number of films being made continued to increase, it became necessary to have professional scenario-writers. Most of the studios did in fact establish their own training schools, in each of which ten to twenty young men worked on making film scenarios and trained as script-writers in the process.

However, no corresponding facilities were provided for film directing. Aspirants continued to learn by assisting the film director. These assistants were usually enthusiastic, but the teaching was incomplete, and they just had to wait and hope. The same applied to prospective cameramen. An assistant's talent became known only if and when he finally got the chance to make his first film. In a Japanese film industry dominated by a small number of major companies, this apprentice-type system still persists today.

However, Akira Kurosawa, internationally renowned for such films as *Rashoman* and *Seven Samurai*, was well known in Japan even when he was only an assistant director. He began writing scenarios which were published in the *Scenario* magazine and were praised by directors. He explains how he did this in an attempt to have his talent recognized faster than was possible under the studio system. Even so, he did not get his first chance to direct until he was thirty-three. This is neither particularly early or late for directors in Japan, simply because there is no earlier recognition; all must wait in the same way. Akira Kurosawa at first studied to become a painter, and by the time he was 18, his paintings had won prizes at major exhibitions. He entered the film world by chance. If he had continued painting, he would certainly have won celebrity sooner than he did by his films.

The film world thus failed by neglect to encourage and train the technicians it dearly needs. The film schools alone made an organized effort to educate and train film-makers.

The first film school in Japan

It was impossible even in the 1920s to study film in any 'school' in Japan. Colleges offered courses in fine arts and art in general, but there were no classes on film. An occasional student might write a graduation thesis on a subject connected with the art of the film, but these were viewed with suspicion by the professors.

The first to offer a professional course in film was Nihon University which, in 1931, also became the first in Japan to have film producing facilities. It established a three-year course in film art; the course was preceded by the actual making of films with 35-mm cameras and recording equipment. In 1939 the Art Department moved to its new campus and built a studio and film processing laboratory. Students had previously made documentaries; now teaching included dramatic films as well, using their own scenarios, photography, film development, and sound recording. These arrangements are still in use.

Most of the graduates joined the major film-making companies; technically qualified graduates were especially welcomed. Those who aspired to become directors, however, had to take their places at the back of the line of junior directors, so to speak, just like graduates of any other university, because of the inflexibility of the apprenticeship system.

As part of the reform of the Japanese educational system in 1949, the Art Department was raised to the status of a four-year College of Arts (on the American model) with film as one of the majors. The number of students increased, facilities were extended, the staff was enlarged, the curriculum was revised, student film-making became better organized, and the whole educational programme was arranged on a step-by-step learning basis.

Today's Film Department

The College of Arts of Nihon University today has a campus in western Tokyo separate from the university's ten other colleges.

In this pleasant environment, relations with those studying other disciplines (fine arts, literature, music, photography, and radio and television) are very much encouraged. Students of film animation, for example, take fine arts classes in painting and sketching and *vice versa*. Future collaboration on these lines will include the joint production of film television commercials.

The Film Department has roughly 500 undergraduates. Of these, 160 are first-year students, while 120 are in the fourth year. The reason for this significant rate of natural elimination is partly that, prior to entering college, would-be students of film have had little opportunity to find out whether they have either talent or a real interest in film. Practical (although fairly simple) exercises in film-making imposed as from the first year soon help students to find out the real extent of their interest, if not of their talent as well.

The possibility of introducing film as an optional subject in secondary schools throughout Japan is being considered, together with the idea of establishing a special three-year secondary-school film course, such as those which now exist for fine arts and music students, who are allowed to combine a minimal academic programme with artistic studies. The purpose, of course, would be to develop the student's sensitivity to the film medium while he is young. No practical steps have yet been taken, however, to establish such a programme.

There is also a proposal to expand and publicize the Film Department's small post-graduate programme which enables a handful of serious students (usually graduates of the college) to continue their studies, working closely with a particular professor. While they may also take undergraduate film classes outside their own undergraduate film speciality, no special post-graduate courses are yet available, and most post-graduate work consists of supervised independent film-making practice, or research.

It is thought that there may be a real need for a more formalized graduate programme which would also cater for graduates (in, for example, literature, fine arts, communication) of other universities who had shown interest and done previous study in films or perhaps attempted independent film-making. The emphasis would be on applied aspects of film-making, since theoretical courses are available at post-graduate level in other universities. However, Ministry of Education regulations which institutions have to satisfy before being allowed to grant graduate degrees make the establishment of an official graduate school somewhat problematic.

The Film Department always has a small number of foreign students, usually from Hong Kong. The teaching staff assist foreign scholars doing research in Japan—arranging meetings, film showings, and access to materials in the college library.

The staff consists of six professors, two assistant professors, and twenty-five instructors, some of whom (for example the psychology instructor who lectures on the psychology of visual perception) teach primarily at other colleges. Others include an executive of a major distributor of foreign films who talks on commercial aspects (for example advertising and promotion, censorship, film financing); an artist from Japan's largest studio working on animated films for both television and cinema; a leading composer of screen music. Well-known directors often give lectures in conjunction with a showing of their films.

When students submit their films for comment and criticism before the panel of Film Department professors, they face men of various ages and of various attitudes and dispositions toward film—from the very conservative to the experimental, from those who regard film primarily as an art to those whose experience in the industry makes them tend to think in terms of ability to communicate and appeal to the average film audience.

The largest class (film appreciation and criticism), compulsory for first- and second-year students, has an attendance of about 300. A few others may have an attendance of about 150, but the average class size is around 20, and the many seminar-type classes have perhaps only 3–10 students each.

All film students take the following classes: basic principles of film art, history of Japanese film, history of foreign film, film appreciation and criticism, research in film works, and methods of scenario expression. In addition, specialized classes are taken according to which of six courses (majors) students choose to pursue.

The film theory and criticism course, following a study of fundamental theories of art and film, includes an analysis of the work of major foreign and Japanese directors, and practice in film criticism. It is intended for prospective film critics and others who need an artistic understanding of film. The practical exercises seek to develop each student's personal qualities and skills.

Interest in the film image (visual expression) course and the social requirements of this age of visual communication was stimulated by the *Expo '70* exhibition held in Osaka in 1970. Film Department professors co-operated in making some of the unique visual displays. The need for skilled artists capable of handling new means of visual expression (for example 360° projection) became very apparent. Starting from a general examination of theories of art, information and communication, and film, the programme proceeds, after dealing with the fundamentals of image composition, to the design and production of documentary, commercial, and animation films and visual displays. Basic classes include history in film theory, fundamentals of image theory and practical exercises in image techniques.

The film photography and sound recording course includes a basic study of related disciplines; fundamental drills (technical compositions in sound or film); and a programme of individualized practical exercises coupled with group projects (done in conjunction with students of the directing and acting courses). The aim is to cultivate the student's powers of expression and qualify him as a sound or photography (camera and lighting) specialist. During the first three years all students take photographic optics, chemistry of film development and sensitometry, physics for film students, film photography (camera work, lenses, filters, sensitometry, studio lighting, etc.), and sound technique (theory of acoustics, recording, mixing and synchronization, etc.). During the fourth year, they specialize as either photographers or sound technicians, actual film-making in consultation with the professors.

Post-synchronization of dialogue in the sound studio.
[Photo: Nihon University, Tokyo.]

Editing room. [Photo: Nihon University, Tokyo.]

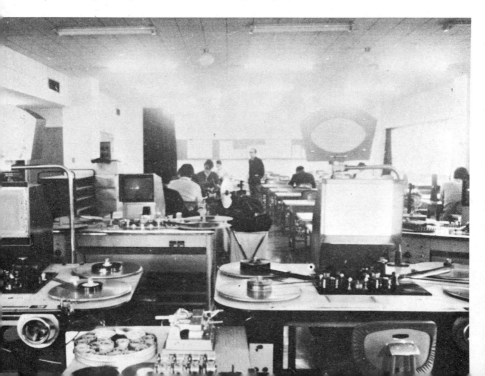

The final course, film acting, includes elocution and physical training (Western and Japanese dance, including formalized traditional sword play). Students study stage acting and the special techniques needed in film and television (for example the large close-up, which may focus attention on the subtle movement of an eyelid). They, of course, act in student film productions. To cultivate the ability to grasp an author's intention from a script, they also study the principles of play and scenario-writing. Basic classes: acting practice, articulation, dance (Japanese and Western) and music.

Each year several special seminars are offered which any student may elect to take. While the selection varies each year, typical subjects are animation, colour sensitometry, documentary film, revival of storytelling in films, or the works of a famous director (for example Kurosawa, Ozu, Mizoguchi, Griffith).

Most fourth-year study is centred around the graduation projects which are required of all students. Students of the film theory and criticism course write a thesis. In other courses, a creative project is usually done as a team effort with other students who function as scenario-writer, director, photographer, sound technician, and 'leading actors'. Students of the film image course may submit either a creative project or a thesis.

Typical graduation projects are 20- to 30-minute black-and-white 16-mm films with synchronized optical sound, including dialogue, sound effects, and music. Students are encouraged to make short films—clearly planned, cleverly executed, carefully edited—and no premium is placed on length. Students bear the cost of film and other incidentals involved in their projects, but all of the Film Department equipment may be used free of charge.

From the second year, students do their own film developing and printing. Processing machines for both black-and-white and colour are available, but few students make colour films because of the expense. Chemicals are prepared in an adjacent laboratory. There are six printing machines, a densitometer to allow accurate correction during printing, and a sensitometer for measuring film curves.

Jobs

The major film companies are having problems which are discussed later. Graduates of the Film Department have recently been entering the 200 or so companies which produce some 1,000 shorts—mostly public relations films—a year. Other firms specialize in educational films to be sold to schools (based on school texts and produced after discussions with educators) or used by various government offices for social education. Each year about 300 such films are produced.

Students interested in making dramatic or documentary films often enter companies which specialize in films for television, while a large section of the film industry is engaged in making commercial shorts for cinema or television projection.

Exchanges

Following various exchanges of visits, the Film Department is planning an exchange of student films with an American university: the best Japanese student films (from amateurs in many parts of Japan) against a similar American package—showings to be arranged in each case to colleges throughout the borrowing country.

Arranging an exchange of actual students is more complicated, since the foreign students would have to know Japanese. It might be possible with some of the larger American universities which have expressed interest and teach both film and Japanese. Nihon University is strongly in favour and has adopted a very flexible and adaptable attitude, but curriculum and other problems still seem to stand in the way of finding a suitable foreign university to act as partner in such an exchange.

Film education at other universities

Of late, several Japanese universities have begun offering film courses, usually within their drama departments. Serious students of film can concentrate on film and write a graduation thesis on the subject. Courses deal primarily with film theory, history, criticism and analysis, but colleges can rarely screen the films discussed. Most do not have proper projection facilities, and even those which do find it difficult for various reasons to borrow foreign classics, or even Japanese films, for screening. Nihon University College of Arts is as yet the only college to have its own film library.

Nevertheless, several graduates from such courses have become famous as directors or as independent film-makers. None of the colleges had the facilities to allow students to practise film-making until recently, when two or three universities have made good the gap.

One example is the Kyushu Art Technology University, a national institution founded in April 1948, and composed of

A lecture on lighting. [Photo: Nihon University, Tokyo.]

The sound stage. [Photo: Nihon University, Tokyo.]

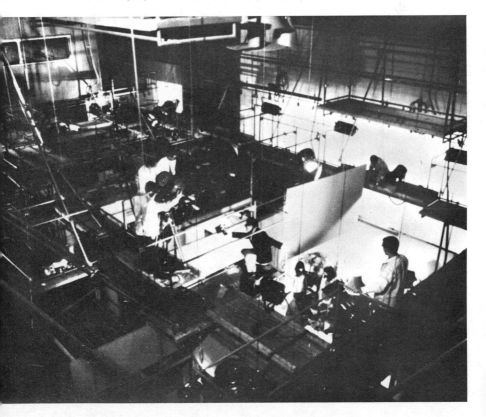

four departments: environmental design, industrial design, acoustic design, and visual design (which includes film and television). Even some of the course titles are new to Japan. For example, the Visual Design Department offers courses in cultural history of image (visual arts), theory of visual communication, theory of moving image design, and image design (applied practice, which covers the making of films and television programmes). However, the content is not really so different from what is offered elsewhere under more conventional titles.

In 1972 the university appointed a full-time professor to the Visual Design Department: Mr Yutaka Yoshima, who has worked as a script-writer for the Tokyo Cinema Company, known world-wide for its scientific films. Mr Yoshima has won several international prizes for his scientific films. He is one of a small number of truly excellent film-makers the university could have invited to become a full-time professor.

Neither the staff nor the facilities of Kyushu Art Technology University are yet complete. The university itself does not expect to reach the standard it is aiming at for perhaps another ten years, mainly because of the difficulty of finding people sufficiently qualified in matters of film and art, and at the same time fully competent to teach.

At this university, film will be treated primarily as a communication medium, to be used mainly for sociocultural purposes; film-makers will be trained to do their own camera work and their directing, and will produce social documentaries rather than dramatic films.

At several universities which have large numbers of students of painting, sculpture, and (recently) design, film has been introduced into the curriculum and basic, if limited, film-making facilities and equipment have been provided. The purpose, however, is not to train future film-makers, but to give the art student some experience of film-making as another of the various art media.

Finally, mention must be made of the Scenario Study Centre, a subsidiary of the Scenario Writers Association (which is made up of professional scenario-writers). Through the association's monthly publication, *Scenario*, professional writers were able to advise amateurs on their work. As this hardly proved adequate, the association established the centre in 1957, as a kind of school for young scenario-writers.

It was at first comparatively small scale, offering half-year courses for some hundred students at a time. The instructors were professional scenario-writers, film directors or critics. However, although most of the instructors were indeed professionals in scenario-writing, their ability to teach was not always adequate. Students did not have time to reach the level of being actually able to write scenarios, but could learn how to go about the job. Several became professional scenario-writers years later, and probably more than twenty are well known by now. These were usually students who had met a professional during the course under whose guidance they continued to study and write.

The Scenario Study Centre has now got a professional course—which resembles an apprenticeship system—for students who want to study beyond the initial half year. The centre will certainly continue to produce fine writers for cinema and television.

Current problems

Film students often take short-term part-time jobs while studying, but some colleges prefer to steer students away from longer term film-related work until they graduate. Too often, an offer from a major studio is sufficient to tempt a student away from his studies, which after all do have their boring aspects. Dropping out, he usually discovers too late that it would have been better to have persevered until graduation.

The Ministry of Education demands certain general education requirements in all colleges which award bachelor degrees. Students who become discouraged are usually those so interested in film-making that their general education subjects, equally necessary for graduation, suffer and they fall academically behind.

Film graduates have recently not been entering the decreasing number of major film companies because of financial stringency in these companies, and also because they still insist on long apprenticeships which mean that, no matter how thoroughly he has studied film, the newcomer must start at the bottom, doing the most menial kinds of work.

Private universities such as Nihon charge high fees which are beyond the capacity to pay of some serious students, however intense their interest in film may be. Opinion is growing in favour of government support for private universities to help in such cases, but little actual progress has been made.

Outstanding films are required by film schools, not only for study purposes but also as a means of inspiring and cultivating gifts of students. But copies for use in this way by universities are extremely difficult to obtain because of copyright problems.

Young people who go into film tend to have a strong taste for free and undisciplined expression—their preoccupation with experimental or underground films sometimes, in fact, borders on the fanatic. One danger in becoming too dogmatic in this way is they will not be able to find a place in the established film world. Curricula should therefore be designed to ensure that the student understands the special role of film in mass communication as well as its experimental possibilities.

The mass education of artists will always be difficult. At the same time, the society of today is demanding more and more 'image experts'. Finding the best curriculum to meet this need demands continual thought and very considerable flexibility.

A new language

As a new language, film is socially and culturally important.

A film was originally regarded only as entertainment, and occasionally as a possible work of art. But today film has taken on various other functions. It was *Expo '70* that made people in Japan aware of the leading role played in visual display by the many forms of film projection including multi-screen techniques. Visitors were continually immersed in images.

Film had come out of the movie theatre, so to speak. The television screen brought it into the family living-room, both as art and as entertainment. Through news reporting, documentation, advertising, it has become a new medium of information and propaganda. More important still, since it escaped from the confines of the movie theatre, film has become a giant of mass communications.

Its role in education has increased too. The scientific film is a new witness and a new recorder at hospitals and research centres. Even for amateurs, film is taking a new shape as a means of obtaining and filing individual documentation. For the salesman, it is a new instrument for persuading customers.

People spend most of their growing lives learning words and language. In this age of visual communication, educational programmes for future image-makers must be more carefully planned, and they must be differentiated for students of the various types of image creation. Makers of artistic films are needed, of course, but there are also news and documentary film-makers to be considered, and still another kind of education is probably necessary for future producers of commercial films (just as language can be taught, but poets, journalists, and advertising copywriters each need their own variations of language use).

It is perhaps no longer enough to think simply of teaching

'film' at a film school. As 'image' or 'film' becomes our second language, it will be necessary to teach students the various aspects of this visual language from an early age. The inclusion of training in image creation, even at the compulsory education level, may become a necessity, not of the distant future, but of education tomorrow.

Manuel González Casanova

Mexico

For many years film-lovers campaigned to have the cinema
recognized as a new art, reasoning that it was the art of arts,
'the seventh art'. On the other hand, its detractors argued that
it was the product of a machine that mirrored reality, a machine
they looked down upon as merely popular entertainment, a
village peep show.

The cinema was eventually recognized as a new art form,
a new language with which it is possible to create, and lie about
or explore reality, and not merely act as its faithful mirror.
However, the contempt remained in academic and intellectual
circles—not always an open, recognized contempt so much as
a condescending attitude, coloured by memories of youthful
pleasures and superficial references to 'the shining and sinful
world of the movies', and a vague idea that audio-visual media
should be useful for teaching purposes.

Cinema as education

Many studies have discussed the importance of film as an educational aid, but little has been done in practice. Most institutions that really believe in the educational value of cinema limit
themselves to documentaries and didactic films, completely
ignoring entertainment cinema. They thoughtlessly regard the
didactic cinema as the only one that educates and fail to notice
the untapped educational potential of the commercial cinema.
The loss is evident if we compare the numbers who attend both

kinds of cinema. Why do we not avail ourselves of this leisure time to educate? Why do we not educate while entertaining?

Through present-day cinema, man is in fact being given an education, he is being taught to live: he is being conditioned to respond to interests that manipulate the cinema industry; he is transformed into a better consumer; he is being accustomed to violence, he is being conditioned to a belief in the 'natural superiority' of a race or he is merely being helped to evade reality. How many intellectuals who despise the movies are being affected in their personal lives by what they scorn? The influence of the movies in human habits is evident in fashion, but what about behavioural fads? Up to what point is the cinema responsible for the breakdown of the institution of marriage? Or the paths followed by the rebellion of youth?

Why do we not utilize the cinema to teach standards of behaviour that are in harmony with the highest ethical principles? The question here is not moralistic, but rather that of making a highly ethical cinema, a cinema that responds to the reality of contemporary man, a cinema which does not deform but which contributes to the new man, able to cope with today's world.

The first step necessary to transform cinema is to change the man who makes it. It is not possible to think in terms of a cinema that responds to the highest interests of humanity with the men that make up the movie industry today since (and I am specifically referring to my country but I believe that the state of the art is more or less the same in other parts of the world) most of the people in this industry have very low cultural standards or are deformed by commercial interests—the wrong bases upon which to create a new type of cinema.

This is why I believe that a film school at university level is so important. If we are to shape the men and women who in turn will contribute to the shaping of millions of people, it is necessary to give them the highest university training possible. It is necessary that they become aware of their responsibility vis-à-vis humanity. It is no longer possible to believe that we are merely training technicians when we train movie-makers. They are certainly technicians but they are also teachers and they must be prepared for and aware of their responsibilities. It is up to us.

Latin America has one of the highest illiteracy rates in the world and the main spiritual and cultural nutrients (not to say the only ones) of the masses are films and television and, specifically, films supplied by the Mexican cinema industry. This is why we have a tremendous responsibility in the training of future film-makers.

It is up to us to decide whether to make an entertainment

cinema that helps to raise the social and cultural standards of our people in America, or to continue to brutalize them through a cinema that gives a false picture of our social reality by extolling *machismo* and violence, prostitution and vice. We wish to make a cinema that contributes to the economic development of our people, and not a cinema that makes them victims of the consumer society. It should be a cinema that teaches them to think, to reason; a cinema that shows them how the world in which we live really is, how men from other parts of the world are; how their problems are, basically, the problems of all men. At this time when the world has become so small, thanks partly to the movies and television, we wish to train film-makers who are conscious of their responsibility, who are interested in encouraging, through their films, the knowledge of man and, therefore, the knowledge of different peoples, as a way to contribute to world peace.

Problems of film education in Mexico

The first attempt to teach film-making in Mexico was made by the Cinematographic Production Workers Union when they created a school to train film technicians. This school, an offshoot of a labour union, did not last long. Founded in the 1940s, it disappeared very quickly because all those who joined it wanted, with the help of their union, to form a part of the national industry.

In 1958, in the Ibero-American University (a private educational institution headed by the Jesuits), a film school was founded which was later absorbed into the Communications Sciences and Techniques Department in the same university.

In the National Autonomous University of Mexico, the first attempt to systematize the teaching of film-making was a short course called 'fifty lessons in film-making', through which we analysed the problems involved in creating a movie, from the script to the editing. The different creative aspects were examined by specialists who, in two or three lectures, analysed their methods of working. This course was rounded off with a series of illustrated lectures on the history of the cinema.

This short course was held in 1960. The following year a new approach to film teaching was adopted. We chose a picture considered to be one of the most important ones in Mexican film-making and invited the film-maker to analyse it in five lectures, and to explain to the students the main problems he had faced. This experience was repeated several times, widening its scope to include an analysis by specialists of the classics of world cinema.

Staff and students in production.
[Photo: University of Mexico.]

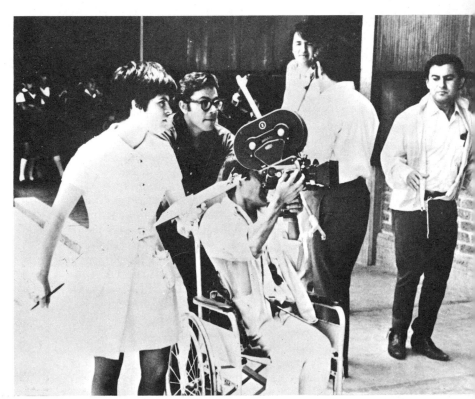

Shooting on location. [Photo: University of Mexico.]

These first attempts led us to found, in 1963, the University Centre of Cinematographic Studies, starting from zero point. Our whole experience was limited to the organization of the short courses just mentioned. We had a very slender budget that was barely enough to pay token fees to the teachers. We did not have technical facilities nor did we have a building of our own, since classes were taught in the science faculty when the science classes were over.

The two main problems have been the lack of resources and the lack of teachers. Since no teachers were available, we had to persuade the professionals who were most willing to become teachers. This was difficult, since most of them had no professional academic training. They were self-made technicians, with no experience of teaching. Many of the technicians who so kindly offered to help had to give up their classes after an initial attempt, since they felt it was impossible for them to go on. Throughout these years our main effort has been to build up a corps of professors, which is something we have been achieving gradually.

To make up the first syllabus, we studied the prospectuses of different established schools, adapting them to our needs and, above all, to our resources.

The lack of resources meant that teaching, during the first few years, had to be rather verbal, dealing with aesthetic rather than technical problems. Our first students had a training that made them more apt as movie critics than as movie-makers. But since our intention was to train film-makers, we went on struggling to obtain enough resources to be able to teach the technical aspects of film-making.

Without having a camera, it is impossible to teach students how to handle one. To teach techniques it is absolutely necessary to have equipment, without which things are half-done and the student becomes frustrated, likely to give up his studies.

During the first few years, the drop-out rate was very high. The second group of students almost disappeared, and we were forced to continue the following year with the only three remaining. Except for this second group, the drop-out rate during the first few years was a little over 50 per cent during the first year, decreasing to 10 per cent more or less as of the second year. In all 25–30 per cent of the registered students completed their studies.

In the group that has just finished their studies, during the first year the drop-out rate went down considerably, since 100 per cent of the registered students took examinations at the end of the year.

We believe this change is due to the change of the academic status of the University Centre of Cinematographic Studies; to the change in the syllabus that included more guided practical work; to a noticeable improvement in our budget and to the nature of the admission examination, which was changed to favour candidates with a more technical background.

From its inception, the centre imposed an entrance examination. During the first year, there were sixty candidates, of whom thirty were admitted. A high percentage were adults. Many of them had been failures elsewhere and some had a certain artistic background. Preference was given to those with the highest educational level, and those who had previous knowledge of the cinema or some other art. Ten students of this group finished their studies, and immediately got jobs (in the film-making industry or in television).

The second group consisted mainly of people who were beginning to make a name in art (including a musician, a novelist, a theatre director). Of these, only three, the least ambitious, completed their studies.

The composition of succeeding groups kept changing as the number of candidates increased. There was a new type of student, generally younger. Almost all of them studied some other university discipline at the same time, or had dropped out of some other professional course.

The number of students admitted during 1970 went down to twenty during the first year, and as of this year we started noticing what was to become a feature of the latest group to be admitted, i.e. most of the students entered directly from high school. In the last group, 190 candidates sat for the entrance examination, of whom twenty were admitted.

One of the most serious teaching problems is the attitude of students to the syllabus, a problem encountered in many parts of the world during the last few years. Student dissatisfaction with a programme that does not meet their needs is aggravated in a new school by a certain lack of trust. Since there is no group of graduates who have made a name for themselves as to underwrite the efficiency of the school, the student is afraid that he is wasting his time in difficult studies that may lead to nothing. The main concern of people who join film schools is to make films, and to start making them quickly.

Students trying to learn film-making face the same problems as arise in other arts, and especially in the theatre. The student has a very vague notion of what he wants to learn. Some are attracted by the glamour that publicity gives to cinema; others believe they have talent and the ability to prove it. The vanity and confusion that characterizes film-making compounds the problem. We have started to fight this by laying the emphasis on techniques, striving to play down the art aspect. We try to inculcate modesty in our students, an attitude that allows

Shooting an outdoor scene. [Photo: University of Mexico.]

them to be good artisans so that, when talent is truly present, it will find expression in cinema language. Since 1970, improved resources have allowed us to enlarge the scope of practical work which students can undertake.

The first practical assignment is a personal, 5-minute film. At the end of the semester, students are given the equipment necessary to 'make a picture'.

Experience has taught us that all students who register in the school already have a picture in mind, and their main concern is to make it. A student wishes to prove himself, to express himself. This is why we have established this custom of allowing him to make it and get it off his mind. Generally speaking, he then becomes more patient about the tedious process of learning techniques. Very often, the student gives the impression that once he has made his film, he is empty, with nothing to say. This sometimes causes him to drop out, which may be a good thing, since it has allowed him to discover that he has nothing to say in the cinema; he has released his restlessness and has finished with his need for cinema expression. He has understood that his is another path and he withdraws. On the other hand, for most students this experience makes them understand more clearly how difficult it is to express themselves through the cinema while they still lack the necessary technical command; they then find it easier to accept having to learn and do exercises. During the second semester the student must make two 7-minute films; the technical requirements imposed start him on the way to acquiring the knowledge he needs as a film-maker.

The first year is for us a screening procedure. It is a continuation of the selection procedure that started with the entrance examination. The entrance examination has been one of our main concerns. Because of the high cost per student of movie-teaching, it is not possible to accept all candidates, and we must choose the most able ones: those who really have a vocation and ability. We must fully test all those who aspire to film-making. But how can we determine who is fit? The greater the number of people who hear about the film school, the greater the number of candidates. What attracts these candidates? In many cases, it is young people attracted by the publicity that surrounds the film industry; youngsters who believe that the cinema is a quick way to make money, besides being something easy and pleasant. There are others who seek a means of personal expression, but lack the will and discipline required of film professionals. Some lack the minimum background necessary to follow lessons at a university level and others simply do not know what they want. They seek admission to the school just as they might to the schools of engineering or law. They wish to do something but have not, as yet, found their true vocation. A few, very few, are truly interested in films, have the necessary qualities and, above all, are perfectly ready to submit to the discipline needed to learn the techniques involved. This ambition will help them overcome all the obstacles, and make movies in spite of lack of money, learn in spite of the deficiencies in the teaching available.

How can we discover this type of student amongst an unlimited number of candidates? How can we distinguish true enthusiasm from the enthusiasm all candidates seem to have? This has been a problem that we have not been able to solve satisfactorily. The decrease in drop-out rates in the last few years has made us feel that we are on the right path when we give greater importance to the technical capabilities of candidates during the admission examination, but we are not quite satisfied; perhaps we may have allowed some exceptional talent to be rejected.

The best way is probably to maintain contact with the student before accepting him for admission. As we need auxiliary technicians in different movie-making branches, we are working with the university authorities with a view to starting a basic programme at upper high school level in the College of Sciences and Humanities of the National Autonomous University of Mexico.

Without any such clear-cut purpose, the teaching of film-making in different buildings of the National Preparatory School (upper high school) began quite a few years ago. In 1960, a class on cinematographic culture (which was introduced as an optional subject) became a cine-club. This subject was taught in different schools without a fixed programme for some years, but was intended as entertainment for adolescents and not cinema training, mostly by professors who regard films as an entertaining pastime. In 1969, the University Centre for Cinematographic Studies requested the National Preparatory School authorities to have the subject taught by graduates from the centre, as part of a common programme for all schools entitled Cinematographic Appreciation. Since 1970, the centre has been responsible for the teaching of photography in the National Preparatory School. This subject was previously taught on a regular basis but in the same manner as the cinema class (without a standard programme), and most teachers also considered it as a hobby.

The participation of centre graduates in the teaching of photography and cinematographic appreciation in upper high school will mean a change in the background that candidates who wish to join our school will have. Our participation in the College of Sciences and Humanities (a new type of upper high school that is being developed in Mexico) will be even more

A boat gives a good vantage point.
[Photo: University of Mexico.]

important, since we are striving to train auxiliary technicians in different branches of cinematographic production—not simply working with stills and elementary ideas about film aesthetics, but systematically training as auxiliary technicians.

These types of studies will also provide a useful outlet for many young people who are merely interested in some aspect of film technique (generally photography), sometimes as in some other occupation. It will also train people who have a minimum cultural background to speak the language of future movie-makers and make it easier for us to choose candidates who are more likely to persevere.

When and if this point is reached, the centre will be revised to take account of previous training acquired by our new students.

The present programme is in four stages, each lasting a year, common to all groups, and a fifth specialization stage of indefinite duration. The fourth and fifth stages have been used at times to make good deficiencies in the training of students of earlier intakes. Apart from teaching problems and the lack of materials, these deficiencies were caused by the total standstill of activities in 1968 and by the aftermath in 1969, when internal agitation and confusion practically paralysed the school.

The four-year, common programme provides a comprehensive training for the future film-maker which will allow him to specialize as he wishes later in any particular branch. Previously, no general training of this nature had been available.

In addition, specialization programmes are being provided for students who finish the fourth stage, outside professionals, and graduates from earlier groups.

Financial problems and support

Lastly, I would like to briefly refer to the main problems that the school has had to face: the lack of resources and the lack of professionally trained teachers.

The school depends, academically and administratively, on the National Autonomous University of Mexico, and its budget until recently formed part of the budget of the University Department of Cinematographic Activities. The school's budget was increased very gradually. The school has now become administratively independent and it received a substantial increase that brings in a little over ten times its original budget—which does not mean much ($1,676,561) but certainly allows us to work better.

In view of the high cost of keeping up the school, and the difficulty of getting increased funds from the university, we have been trying to generate our own resources. We are producing feature films made entirely by people from the school, and have started organizing small projection rooms, mainly relying on the universities in different parts of Mexico. These showings should create a new source of income.

The other problem, the lack of professionally trained teachers, is one we have been solving as we go along, first by employing technicians as teachers, and people who have trained abroad (mainly in Europe). Our experience with the latter has generally been unfavourable. They had been absent from their own country for such long periods before achieving personal maturity, and found it difficult to adapt themselves to the environment and working conditions in Mexico. Barely 10 per cent of those recruited have been able to continue as teachers in our school. We therefore have little desire to help young students without previous local training to go abroad to study film-making—not until they have studied at least up to third year in the University Centre for Cinematographic Studies. On the other hand, I do believe that scholarships to allow specialized training for our teachers or for graduates who might later be able to teach would certainly be useful.

Some of the earlier and most capable graduates are now teaching at the centre. This process has certain limitations, but in our case it is absolutely unavoidable. Most of these teachers make up for their lack of experience and the weak points in their education by being youthfully enthusiastic, and their easier relations with new groups of students leads to better academic training.

Bertil Lauritzen

Sweden

The organized education of film-makers, although it has existed in Sweden for less than ten years, has had considerable success, but the aims as well as the methods are still under discussion among organizers, teachers and students. There are differences of opinion regarding the need to change certain traditional structures in society, different views on culture in Sweden, different definitions of such words as art, communication and professionalism, different views on the trends of technical development and the role of film in the society of tomorrow.

This article is concerned with the trends and ideas involved, rather than with providing a detailed description of the actual training structure.

Background

The political implications of cinema were frequently discussed in Sweden during the 1950s. Previously, public interest had been mainly concerned with the film industry and such questions as entertainment tax and censorship. The arrival of television made the debate on these restrictive factors more acute; at the same time, there was a growing demand for more positive educational action.

The Swedish Film Academy proposed in 1960 that film should be accepted as a 'full member of the cultural society' both as an art form and as a medium of communication, and be included in the general educational system on three levels: in primary and secondary schools with the same status as languages or aesthetic subjects; in the film equivalent of conservatories for music and pictorial arts; film courses and research in the universities.

In 1963, the State signed an agreement with the film trade, abolishing the entertainment tax on cinemas, and establishing a foundation (the Swedish Film Institute) which was to be jointly administered, financed by a 10 per cent share of practically all cinema receipts, and was to foster 'Swedish film culture' and organize the education of film-makers. A film school was accordingly started in 1964. With the financial assistance of the institute, a film faculty was established in Stockholm University in 1970. The teaching of film became part of the compulsory curricula of primary and secondary schools as from the middle of the 1960s.

The creation of the Swedish Film Institute formed part of the governmental policy of cultural democratization in the arts by improving educational possibilities and living conditions for the professional artist, and providing more equitable access (geographical as well as social) for the public.

It was then found that educational facilities for creative staff were unsatisfactory not only in film but also in theatre, radio and television. The theatre only had actors' schools, radio and television had nothing except some internal courses for staff of the monopolistic, semi-governmental Swedish Broadcasting Corporation.

Various reasons were advanced in favour of providing a co-ordinated system of education valid for theatre, film, radio and television. Most production functions are parallel in all four so that, in a small country like Sweden, the range of employment openings is widened by an education in basic techniques that can be adapted to several media; so also is the freedom of the creative artist to choose the medium he finds best suited for a particular subject or in reaching a particular audience.

The governmental Swedish Dramatic Institute was accordingly established in 1970 to provide education in theatre, film, radio and television, and to replace or take over the activities of the film school of the Swedish Film Institute, which was then discontinued.

Film school of the Swedish Film Institute

Since both the film school and the Swedish Film Institute were financed from cinema admission charges, training criteria were nationally influenced by the idea of making successful films for cinema distribution; and since cinemas provide the normal distribution channel for film art, artistic ambitions were legitimate criteria of 'quality' in film production.

After studies of several reputed film schools abroad, it was decided to concentrate in the school on practical film work which, of course, is much more expensive than just providing classes. However, by limiting the studies to two years, the budget per student and year could be rather generous without extending the costs per graduate (as compared with schools having courses lasting three to five years).

It was then decided that the school should offer training in a nucleus of the creative contributions to film-making, i.e. for prospective directors, production administrators, cameramen and sound technicians (actors to be trained in specialized schools). This choice again meant going against accepted traditions and prejudices, for the importance of the production manager to the creative capacity of the team is too often neglected, while the sound technician is considered only as a technician, without regard to his creative contributions at various stages. On the other hand script-writing and editing were not treated as separate branches: script-writing was allocated mainly to the curriculum of the director's branch, while editing would be one of a main item of study in all branches.

This professional structure has already had an obvious influence on the composition of teams and the way they co-operate in recent Swedish film production. As there were usually about ten times as many applicants as there were places available, the conditions of admission became a matter of great importance, but they depended on what might be called a qualified guess. Students were admitted between the ages of 20 and 30 years. Results of previous examinations were neither demanded or counted as equivalent to practical creative experience. However, prospective production administrators, cameramen and sound technicians had to prove they had reached a certain level by study and/or practical experience. A certain level of general knowledge was also demanded in all branches, but it was clearly understood that, for instance, an applicant aged 28 could have gained such knowledge otherwise than by passing a matriculation examination ten years earlier.

Selection was in two stages. In a written application, the applicanli replied to certain questions and was free to quote any qutaficacions he considered appropriate. Three to four times as many applicants as there were places available were then invited for interview. Over a period of three to six days, the selection boards were assisted by psychologists to help in clarifying points of special interest in the search for creative talent.

During the first year, students in each branch had specialized courses and periodically joined team exercises. Towards the end of the year, each did his part in producing a short 16-mm film. The second year was organized as a workshop, in which short film productions alternated with seminars and specialized courses.

Despite much justified criticism, these methods had proved successful from the point of view of Swedish film production and of the students themselves. Most of the graduates already have a recognized standing in the profession.

The Swedish Dramatic Institute

The institute offers two years' training in direction, production management, picture technique (camera and lighting), sound technique, make-up and set design.

The institute also provides a one-year course in production methods and techniques in theatre, film, radio and television. This course is open to persons from other professions who to some extent need such qualifications in their ordinary work (for example teachers, journalists, authors, social workers, television specialists). The course concentrates on light-weight production, for example using mobile stage equipment, 8-mm and 16-mm film, light tape recorders, and so on. Students also learn about the work of the different professional sections of the institute.

As from 1973 the institute provided further training in the various specializations covered in the two-year and one-year courses; this training is also open to other categories of people concerned with the specializations in question.

There are an average of twelve applicants for each place available at the institute. The admission procedure is in two stages (as it was at the film school) but is completed without the assistance of psychologists. Selection boards consist of one teacher and one student of the specialization, plus one expert not otherwise connected with the institute. No previous examination qualifications are demanded. Foreign applicants who know a Scandinavian language are treated in the same way as Swedish applicants. The average age of admission is 26 years. The institute has all production facilities required in theatre, film, radio or television. No fees are charged: Swedish students receive the same study grants and loans as university students.

In the two-year courses students may choose to concentrate, from the beginning, on either film and television, or

Students on location.
[Photo: Dramatiska Institutet Filmhuset, Stockholm.]

theatre and radio. This choice takes place during the second year in the case of the make-up and set design courses.

The institute tries to find distribution channels for student productions and arranges audience reaction tests. Since a school can never fully provide ordinary performance conditions it encourages co-operation, sometimes on co-production lines, between students and outside professional groups.

It is also a responsibility of the institute to organize the studies in such a way as to stimulate media development. It welcomes suggestions from students, and sets problems involving content, form, production methods and technique, which students and teachers jointly tackle in experimental teams.

Problems

The education of the film-maker, as hitherto understood in Sweden, raises certain problems which may also arise in other countries and should be considered by anyone planning new institutions for such education.

First, the education of the film-maker has been considered as something separate, having no clear connexion with education in general. It is classified as 'higher education', but without defining the basic education on which it is supposed to build. It is difficult to formulate the curriculum of a course of education when neither the starting-point nor the expected result can be clearly defined; it must itself define an educational level for recruits, and measure what can be achieved, as from that level, against the time and resources at its disposal.

Second, there is the question of the relation of production exercises to the education programme as a whole. If the exercises are exciting and realistic, they may so absorb the students as to distract them from other studies for very long periods during the limited time the course lasts. Again, in making up teams for such exercises, the obligation to offer equal working possibilities for all students may easily conflict with a natural grouping of students that may suggest itself around different project themes. Organizing studies under a given curriculum flexibly enough to suit the creative gifts of the individual students represents another challenge.

Such problems are, however, internal and minor. The question is whether or not a school meets existing or foreseeable needs. On this point there is much debate in Sweden among those concerned with the role and development of film as a social factor.

Questions

The education of the film-maker in Sweden was based on the underlying idea that film is an art form—understandably enough, since the advocates of such education among the film experts themselves fought for decades to get this idea accepted.

This, however, has placed the whole question in the middle of a much wider debate regarding the definition of art itself and its role in the culture of today and tomorrow.

Various definitions of art are possible. It can be defined in terms of content, form, quality, creativity and so on. But in everyday use, any definition can be faulted for non-conformity with some traditional prejudice.

Irrelevant factors are dragged in, for example time and place of the creative act, intended purpose, artistic status of the maker in question and so on. For example, a sermon or a lecture seldom ranks as performing art. Memoirs and travel books may be literature, but not textbooks on history or geography. Apart from Toulouse-Lautrec, few poster designers are referred to as artists.

The same prejudices apply in film. Whole sectors are never mentioned in film history as taught in the universities. For instance, a film produced for educational purposes and distributed directly to schools will almost certainly never be noticed by the pundits, no matter how excellent in quality or how large its audiences.

Should the education of the film-maker be limited to the limited sector of film production which regards film primarily as an art form? This is a regular item in the debate. In a way, the introduction of the one-year course for non-professionals described above constitutes a part answer to the question.

If it is agreed, on the other hand, that the education of the film-maker should cover all the ways in which film is being increasingly used as a means of expression and a medium of communication in modern society, can curricula and courses be devised which are versatile enough to cover the varied production conditions of even the major categories of film?

Will it be possible, around a nucleus of basic techniques for use in film and television, to devise a series of differentiated courses which the student can combine in a way that qualifies him to produce one or more of the categories of film that will be needed in the society of tomorrow?

The size of production teams and the degree of specialization needed within them varies from project to project and from one category of film to another. Can the series of courses then also allow the student to choose between either concentrating on one speciality (for example directing, camera, sound) or taking a balanced but necessarily more elementary course of training in a number of different techniques? Is such flexibility feasible?

Interpretation of professionalism

Professionalism is another basic concept, i.e. the student is supposed to gain enough competence to fill specified posts in the film industry and merit his mention in the credit titles.

Since the organizational structure of film production has been changing rapidly during the last ten years, this traditional concept must also be reconsidered. The Swedish film industry has nowadays practically no production staff on its payrolls. Teams are recruited on a freelance basis and the distribution of responsibilities within the team varies. The film-maker must thus be educated for a freelance labour market. The qualifications necessary are much more difficult to define, as the freelance will normally have to earn his living by working in different categories of film production. Some people feel that an all-round training would suit the freelance situation best, others claim on the contrary that specialization will make the student more competitive. In film production there is certainly a place for both categories.

The professional is traditionally associated with industrialized 35-mm production, ambition and skill. The swift development of substandard production techniques, however, has led to a decentralization of film production, and a growing number of people contribute on a high level of ambition and skill but often earn their living at least partially elsewhere. They are thus neither professional film-makers nor amateurs in the traditional sense of these terms. They are often self-educated so far as film work is concerned, with gaps in their experience that are the result of a lack of resources and guidance. It is hoped that the new short specialized courses referred to earlier will help them to make good these deficiencies.

Communication and cultural democracy

The future education of the film-maker in Sweden will, of course, be influenced by the development of film teaching in the ordinary school system.

As in many other countries, such teaching was originally advocated on aesthetic grounds: as a new art form film should be taught in schools as an addition to the traditional forms. Moreover, teachers, parents and school authorities were aware

Directing students in a studio production.
[Photo: Dramatiska Institutet Filmhuset, Stockholm.]

of the possible adverse influence of film and television on ideas and behaviour and regarded knowledge about the media as the best antidote. Practical film exercises would then be based on the idea that you understand a language better once you have tried to use it. Film knowledge was not a separate subject at first but was included in Swedish art and social science teaching.

At the beginning of the 1960s film was officially included in the curriculum, and another approach was advocated: film should be regarded as a language and taught in schools in the same way as other languages; the teaching should cover both the production and the receiving end of film communication. Secondary-school students can now study film and television three hours a week for two years as part of 'aesthetic specialization', as an alternative to a third foreign language (two foreign languages being compulsory). A similar alternative was later introduced also in the last grade of primary school.

One general objection to this idea (that all Swedish citizens should master the film medium and so be able to participate in the communication process both as receivers and by being able to express their own ideas and experiences) is that it would lead to an unnecessary consumption of equipment and material and that national resources could be used instead in ways that better serve immediate needs.

However, the idea of treating film in schools as a language (with an aesthetic side) seems to have come to stay. Moreover, technical development is making 8-mm film and light-weight electronic equipment about as exotic to the average citizen as a typewriter. The standardization of film and videocassettes may further help the regional and local democratization of communications.

Film teaching in Swedish schools is still at an early stage, being hampered by the lack of competent teachers (for whom training is not yet satisfactorily organized). However, such teaching will eventually create an entirely new situation in regard to the higher education of the film-maker, which will then take its place at the top of a definable educational pyramid.

The education of the film-maker in Sweden has hitherto regarded film as an art and grouped teaching under well-defined categories (director, cameraman, sound technician). This education must now adjust to a changing cultural situation, the changing role of film and film-maker in society, and to changes in technique and production methods.

The introduction of a one-year course for non-professionals is a first adjustment.

The next step will be to decentralize in-service courses for professional film-makers and courses for others who need to know about film and television for the purposes of their work.

Education will have to cater for the makers of socially important categories of film production which are not conventionally classified as art.

The teaching of film in schools and in adult education courses still needs professional assistance but will later furnish a base of recruitment for higher education in film-making.

Should the advanced education of the film-maker be organized, as now, in one school, or decentralized in several? This question is bound to arise eventually. For the moment a slight bias in the direction of decentralization is represented by the short courses in film-making that have already been initiated at universities, journalist high schools, teacher's high schools and audio-visual centres. In several cases, these are turning to the Swedish Dramatic Institute for assistance.

V. Zdan

Union of Soviet Socialist Republics

Two major film schools are responsible for the training of key personnel in the Soviet Union: the National Institute of Film-making (VGIK) for the creative side, and the Institute of Film Engineers (LIKI), in Leningrad, for engineers and technicians.

The VGIK was set up in 1919, the first national film school, and has now been training professionals for over fifty years—scenario-writers, directors (full-length films, documentaries, popular scientific, educational, cartoons, television), directors of photography, actors, set designers, film historians, film critics, film editors, production and distribution managers.

The fact that the professorships are concerned with both teaching and research is important to the creativity of a film school, since film is an essentially synthesizing art. As a manifestation of creative genius, film cannot be created by an isolated artist. It demands team work, and by people who have shared the same common film education (in which they later specialize).

Teaching at the institute allows a continuous moving back and forth between theory and practice during the student's four- to five-year stay.

In art education, it is impossible to separate the creative and artistic from the more technical side. Today's film-making and today's viewers demand the thinking artist, one who is aware of his responsibilities in society and deeply interested in all that is going on; otherwise, a talented artist, overtaken by the great sociopolitical currents of his time, loses touch, and tends to fall back on the same old themes and methods. Our entire experience here proves this.

This inseparable unity of theory and practice is reflected in institute teaching.

The theoretical part of the course fosters the student's artistic gifts, refines his conception of the world, and acquaints him with the laws of social evolution. In order to widen horizons so that students are not limited just to the cinema; and to recall the cultural heritage and explain the development of world culture, we teach them the underlying principles of related arts (notably theatre, literature, music and painting), philosophy, history, aesthetics, psychology and ethics.

The assimilation of the classics of world film and of the related arts shows the student that dogmas become outdated as well as enabling him to see what imperishable art can be made by consciously searching for new forms of expression. Despite all the existing variations in teaching structures, other differences will inevitably arise and must be foreseen if we are to produce thinking and honest artists who can tackle, in a creative and robust way, contemporary artistic and ideological problems.

Institute faculties cover direction and acting, photography, architecture and film set design, scenario-writing, theoretical studies, and film economics. (The Karpenko-Kary Theatre Institute in Kiev has a film course organized on similar lines.)

Directors and actors

In their department, direction and acting each has its separate programme.

The film director is, in a way, the motor behind the efforts of the team. It is he who decides how the film will be composed. He organizes the complex process of film production. He is concerned not only with the artistic and ideological qualities of the work, but also with its financial results.

The student learning how to make a full-length film, studies shooting, film sets, music, sound, composition, interpretation and editing—in short, everything which relates to the production of a film. After a theory course, he starts by composing scenes, and continues to work on dramatic composition until he leaves. He works with actors in studying the art of interpretation. He learns to edit written works, under the direction of teachers, during his first year, and this continues for four years. In the workshops, he works with the great film teachers from the first year to the last; Kuleshov, Eisenstein, Pudovkin, Dovjenko, Savtchenko and Youtkevitch have all worked at VGIK as Guerassimov, Romm, Dsiguane, Stopler, Tchoukhrai, Talankine and others are doing today.

Studies at the workshops are arranged as follows.

Theoretical lectures which deal systematically with staging, production and interpretation.[1]

Seminars in which students present papers and discuss and analyse shots and takes.

Practical classes in direction and interpretation, on the set.

Tutorials which consider each student's practical work and preparations for his diploma, and films produced by student teams in various departments and sections.

At the various stages of making a film (preparing the scenario, adapting it, making a production project, shooting exteriors and interiors, cutting) discussions with students of the various sections concerned (production, adaptation, acting, shooting, painting) are valuable not only in themselves but in making the future producer aware of the necessity of team-work in the production of a film.

The institute has its own studios, and prospective directors start shooting there in their second year. The complexity of the tasks allotted, and of the film length gradually increase: from silent studies (200 m) to shorts (300-900 m) up to full length in the final year (sometimes done by invitation in professional studios).

The actor is central to film-making. There can be discussion about the relative merits of the man who wrote the story and the director but to the average viewer, the actor makes or mars the film. He appears on the screen and takes all the viewer's attention, embodies the film's ideas. He may be asked to play out any role involved in the infinite variety of human relationships and the mazes of human existence. He is both a creator and an instrument, and interpretation is the art that allows him to combine both. In this regard, the work of Stanislavsky is known throughout the world, and the system he elaborated still remains the immutable basis of an actor's training in the Soviet Union.

One essential difference between cinema and theatre is that the camera is not restricted in time and space as it records the actor's behaviour. It can follow his expressions in close-up; the microphone captures the slightest changes of intonation; and the cinema 'eternalizes' his art. Hence the need for exactness, delicacy, attention to details, which would be unimportant in the theatre, where there is always a distance between the actor and the viewer. His technique depends on nuances. No

1. cf. Stanislavsky: '. . . our artistic nature has its own laws of creation. They are valuable for all individuals, for all nations. These laws must be understood. They must constitute the basis of our programs of instruction. They are studied in all their details. There are no other possibilities of training great talents.'

technical process can substitute for this. An artistically true and perfect work depends on the well thought out intentions and the talents of the actor himself.

The actor must consider himself not as the one who carries out the wish of the author or of the director, but as the person who invents the character. He is a co-author of the film, possessing to perfection the instrument of his work—his individual personality.

Experience at VGIK indicates that an actor can be trained not only in actor workshops but also by working with future directors under the direction of a master teacher. The director should know, in theory and from practice, how an actor works, while the actor in turn should understand what the director is trying to do. From the beginning of his studies, the actor at the institute works closely with the director, and they collaborate as equals.

The actor's plan of studies includes: (a) talks by the head of the studio on the general problems of creation for actors and directors; (b) practical work on the set by groups and individuals; (c) independent work by students; (d) experience on film teams led by student directors.

This systematic course develops the actor's physical and psychological powers, his personality, helps him to overcome obstacles, and endows him with initiative, will, imagination, and the ability to use them fully.

Stanislavsky pointed out that, in working with actors, teaching procedures must vary with each individual case, and each time be the object of minute research.[1] This education must be directed by a skilled teacher who, while teaching the classical procedures which everyone needs, is at the same time concentrating on the student's individual artistic potentialities. The training of the film actor resembles that of the stage actor; the artificial separation between the two, so widespread during the era of the silent film, no longer exists.

The actor graduates by creating a role in a play or professional film. His diploma states that he is qualified to play both in the cinema and in the theatre.

Documentary, educational and popular science film is a section in the directing faculty. It trains directors in workshops where they study the working methods of documentary film directors and the technological processes involved. They also study shorts, Soviet news films, and the classics of world documentary.

The curriculum includes: history and theory of the documentary, seminars on key problems, including scenario-writing

1. cf. Stanislavsky, *The Work of the Actor on Himself.*

and composition; shooting; the image of man; documentaries without actors; characteristics of documentaries; television reporting. The actual shooting is done under the direction of chief cameramen and involves: (a) making a short film (100 m); (b) a film on a topical subject, with sound effects (120 m); (c) a film on a subject selected by the student (300 m); (d) degree task: a film (300-600 m) made in the institute studios or in professional or television studios.

The prospective directors of popular science films study and assimilate the working methods of professional producers, and the possibilities of expression of various film-making techniques. They learn how to combine wealth of content with a variety of processes of expression.

Besides the lectures and seminars on film history and theory it is hoped to provide opportunities for students to meet people who have won scientific or cultural renown.

The course for student cameramen includes: (a) shooting a 100-m film report on an event; (b) filming a short popularization for the *Science and Technology* programme (120 m); (c) degree task: making a film (300-600 m) on a scientific subject at the institute, or in professional film studios.

Producers of educational films take much the same course as producers of documentary and popular science films. Educational films for secondary and post-secondary schools need directors who are also teachers and who have kept up with progress in the different subjects (mathematics, physics, chemistry, biology, medicine, and so forth). Hence the film workshop admits people with a post-secondary education who have worked as teachers or done research. The three-year course qualifies producers to make educational films on specific subjects (physics, biology, medicine, agriculture, and so on). The whole question of educational films is at present being discussed from a number of angles, including the following:

How can educational films be classified in relation to subject, age of students, level of training, place in curriculum, educational purpose, use in secondary, post-secondary, television or correspondence course education?

The effectiveness for teaching purposes of various shooting procedures (analysis of the evolution of the observed phenomenon (high speed and time-lapse)), the study of phenomena which escape direct observation (macro-and micro-cinematography, the use of polarized light, ultra-violet and infra-red rays, X-rays, the use of air navigation equipment, underwater photography, and so on).

Possible new uses—programmed instruction, film as an integral part of a lesson transmitted on television, television as an autonomous element in the educational process.

Cameramen

The chief cameraman plays a major role in film and television, one that needs high professional ability, specialized knowledge, and a creative gift. His work involves films of all kinds: feature, documentary, popular science, television. He must combine the qualities of a gifted artist with those of an experienced technician. Modern techniques offer him vast possibilities of expression.

Student cameramen familiarize themselves with the equipment and techniques, beginning with specialized practical classes: photo and optical equipment, photographic materials and methods, lighting techniques, photographic composition.

The major course (the art of the chief cameraman) includes theory and practice and covers: (a) shooting, image, principal forms of expression, composition; (b) lighting, 'painting' with light, lighting of sets in studios and exteriors, natural light, special effects; (c) features preparations before shooting, studios and exteriors, films for television, filmed interviews; (d) documentary (film reporting, television reporting, sports films, documentary films); (e) science films (popular science, instructional research).

At each stage, and in each subject (lighting, composition, film reporting, special photography, superimposed shooting) students meet practical creation and production problems, and so learn the full range of possibilities of expression open to the cameraman, and the relation of camera work to film directing as a whole. In preparing the diploma task, student cameramen work in conjunction with student directors.

The chief cameraman must know how to handle black-and-white and colour, and different film formats (reduced, normal, wide, panoramic). Shooting techniques are being constantly developed and curricula must in consequence vary so as to remain up to date.

Screen writers and critics

The status of the scenario-writer is controversial and uncertain. His role is often reduced to nothing. Nevertheless, the scenario remains the basis of any film. Cinema will continue to require scenarios of high quality, and there will always be a need for specialists in scenario-writing.

The screen-writer needs more than an acquired knowledge of films and film-making. If he has no writing talent he will never succeed, and no school can save him. He must have some literary gifts, and must have acquired a certain experience.

Admission to the institute course is subject to the submission of original writing (short story, narrative, essay).

The film and television script-writing course involves theoretical lectures at the institute, a wide general knowledge, practical experience in film and television scenario editing sections, and preparation of a diploma task. The course is designed to help the student to develop his writing gifts, his artistic imagination and his powers of observation, his ability to select and compare data, to generalize, to hit upon the salient idea, and to acquaint himself with new aspects of life.

The course is based on the following principles.

Assimilation of the art: a deep study of life, moving from local to more complicated problems; the specific problems of film-making; study of national and foreign models of script-writing (both film and television).

An exacting attitude toward the written word as the primary material in the creative process; possibilities of film expression; transformation of content and ideas into film-script terms.

Stimulation of a lively interest in current events, science, culture (national and foreign), art exhibitions, new literature and music.

Co-ordination of literary and film work, i.e. students write essays and scenarios which student producers and cameramen transform into film.

Specialization in specific aspects of script-writing: artistic, documentary, popular scientific. The head of the department assigns students in this way after an assessment of their individual capabilities.

The scenario diploma task (feature film, two or three shorts, or a television scenario) must reflect a good knowledge of modern and artistic life, sound judgement, and an ability to utilize the possibilities of film expression in cinema and television.

Theoretical studies

Specialists in film studies include film historians, aestheticians, and film editors (in cinema and television), and they cover theory and history, criticism and sociology. They are much in demand in many sectors. They teach, do research in specialized schools, studios and film libraries, and help to ensure the accuracy of scenarios and films. They also edit or write for the press, publishing houses, radio and television.

The plan of studies includes general subjects, courses in cinema theory and history, and attempts to tie theory to actual film production, i.e. the student works in the studios as a film and television editor, and then on a newspaper or magazine as a (literary) editor or film critic. The particular kind of training offered changes with changes in film practice and other requirements. Effort was first concentrated on training specialists in film history. Later it shifted to training editors for work in the studios. Now it is concerned with such subjects as 'fundamentals and principles of television', 'television editor', and 'sociology of film'. The course ends, as in the other departments, with a diploma task, dealing with a film, history, or theoretical problem.

Architecture and set design

As Stanislavsky once wrote: 'A set decorator or set designer who works for the theatre must necessarily also be a director, knowing how to utilize the principles of our art, and its techniques.' The same can be said of the film set designer. He must also have the eye of a director and cameraman, since he must understand staging and editing, and be able to see, as the cameraman does, through a frame as if looking with the eye of the moving camera.

The set designer must be able to create for an almost unlimited variety of situations depending upon the film's pictorial background, characters and atmosphere. He must be able to draw, paint and imaginatively envisage the scenes in which the action takes place in the same way as the director imagines the action itself.

The institute has separate set design training studios and workshops for: (a) film directors and cinema set designers; (b) television set designers and directors; (c) set designers of art and science films and television; (d) producers and set designers of cartoons, popular science films and television.

Film and television set designs are worked out in collaboration by the director and the chief cameraman. In the teaching programme, students from the other departments also co-operate.

The film set designer course leads to a diploma. The student must select a theme, give his reasons for selecting it, and plan and carry out his project.

Film economics

Film-making is one of the few arts in which the transformation of imagination into art must be minutely examined in terms of economic accountability. Film is not only art and creation, but also a product, the outcome of a combination of complicated techniques.

Film economists are the organizers of film production in the studios and on television, and also work in the distribution and projection networks. The institute trains economists with specific reference to this film background, acquaints them with the work of directors, cameramen and set designers, and the techniques and technology involved. It teaches them planning, film administration and, in general, how to ensure smooth, efficient production at least cost.

Leningrad Institute

As already indicated, film technicians and engineers are trained at the Institute of Film Engineers (LIKI), in Leningrad. This institute was founded in 1918 and was originally called the Institute of Photography. Its three departments (electrical, mechanical, chemical technology) train the engineering technologists who deal with photo and film materials, sound engineers (sound recording and reproduction) and projection systems engineers. The first professorships were in acoustics, sound techniques, optics, film equipment, production of photo-cinema materials, photography, film processing, and electro-techniques. The staff taught and did research on new systems of fixing the film image and new optical systems; they collaborated with the Institute of Scientific Photo Film Research in multiple screen research.

Other schools

Several schools provide technical film education at secondary level (Leningrad, Rostov, Alma-Ata, Lvov, Voronej, Zagorsk and others) and prepare technicians for work in film and projection installations.

The Soviet Union also has a vast network of special schools and technical institutes for the study of cinema.

Keith Lucas

United Kingdom

Emeritus Professor of Film in the Slade School of Fine Art, Thorold Dickinson, one of the fathers of film education in the United Kingdom, lecturing in 1963, commented that 'the standard opinion of the majority of craftsmen in the British film industry in the 1950s was that the best way to learn a job [to become a film-maker] was to go in [to the film industry] at the bottom and work your way up'. It is certainly true that in the fifties there was very little support for the concept of film schools, either amongst film-makers or educationists. To some extent this prejudice still exists, though the establishment in October 1971 of the National Film School can presumably be taken as a sign that the existing film schools have at long last won this battle and established the validity of film education in the United Kingdom.

To obtain a clear picture of the range of educational opportunities for film and television in the United Kingdom, it is necessary to describe not only the professional schools of film and television production but also the supporting schools and institutions dealing with other aspects of film and television education, such as the British Film Institute and the specialist associations and societies, each of which add to the richness of our film and television culture.

This article sets out the broad context of film and television education in the United Kingdom, describes the major professional schools of production, including the British Broadcasting Corporation (BBC), summarizes the smaller departments which provide one of the main sources of recruitment for the senior schools, and then turns to the supporting institutions dealing with film history and culture. In conclusion, it attempts to draw together these two streams of educational activity and assess the contribution they make to our film and television culture.

Context of film and television education

During the 1960s the United Kingdom saw a continuing reduction in the number of cinemas and cinema attendances. Production of feature films continued to fall while levels of some other forms of film production were maintained and even increased. Television and film-making for television were the most active areas of employment. The feature-film industry had to accommodate itself to changing patterns of finance and control. Many of the large studios were closed, became rental companies or turned to producing film for television. Many of the reduced number of feature films were produced by small production companies, sometimes set up for production of one film only. Television increasingly became the proving ground for directors of feature films. John Schlesinger, Jack Gold, Ken Russell, Peter Watkins, Kevin Billington, Warris Hussain, are examples of directors who moved from television to feature-film direction.

The large studios which had operated before 1939 provided a stability of employment and the opportunity for an apprenticeship system to function. With the exception of the BBC, the closure of many studios left the United Kingdom without any practical means of training the film-makers of the 1940s and 1950s. It was to fill this educational vacuum that a number of film schools were started in the late 1950s.

Major professional schools

The late 1950s and early 1960s saw the foundation of the four major film schools in the United Kingdom. These were the School of Film and Television in the Royal College of Art, the London Film School, the School of Film in the Central London Polytechnic and the School of Film, Television and Radio in the University of Bristol. In addition to these four schools there were the various training schemes run by the BBC, which seen collectively provided within the corporation the equivalent of another major film and television school. These are now joined by the National Film School.

The School of Film and Television
in the Royal College of Art

Founded about ten years ago the school trains for every branch
of film and television. It provides the most comprehensive
range of production experience in both film and television of
any of the schools in the United Kingdom. The Royal College
is a post-graduate university college financed by the State, and
functions under its own Royal Charter and is able to award its
own degrees. The college comprises fourteen schools and departments dealing with every branch of the visual and plastic
arts, and has a number of specialist research departments.
There are over 600 students, mainly supported by State bur-
saries, and studying for a master of arts degree.

The School of Film and Television recruits about twenty
students a year, having a total of about sixty. They come from
universities, colleges of art, technology, drama or music or from
the film or television industries. They normally study for three
years.

The school is divided into seven teaching departments with
supporting technical, maintenance and administration sections.
The teaching departments comprise: television; film camera
and lighting; editing; sound; animation; design; film history.
Each department is run by professionally experienced tutors
and has its own budget to enable it to mount its own teaching
projects and experiments.

Supporting sections include production control and
budgeting; still photography and library.

Normally, tutorial and technical staff work professionally
in film and television in addition to teaching.

The film programme is mainly on 16 mm. The school is
well equipped with a wide range of modern cameras, ten cutting
rooms, viewing and negative cutting rooms, and videotape is
being developed as an aid to editing so that various stages of
the editing process can be recorded and then replayed for the
purpose of comparison. There are full projection facilities, and
professional dubbing and transfer systems capable of dealing
with eight tracks simultaneously. The Animation Department
has an Oxberry for 35 mm and 16 mm and a separate 8-mm
rostrum for 'notebook' work, and has its own design studio.
The Television Department has a three-camera colour television
studio with telecine and caption scanning. The studio has a
working area of about 2,500 ft². The department is equipped
with colour videotape recording with insert editing facility. It is
the only professional colour studio available outside the broadcasting companies for training purposes.

Directing or script-writing activities are encouraged to

emerge naturally from experience gained in the other practical working departments of the school. Tuition in elementary script-writing and direction are given as part of the first year course. Later, specialist work is supervised by individual tutors.

The normal course structure is based on practice. The first year comprises an intensive introduction to techniques. Students are expected to gain a basic understanding of every branch of production work and encouraged to choose areas of further specialized study. The interrelationship of film and tele-vision is an important part of the introductory course. All students undertake work in film history and courses of aes-thetics and philosophy.

Practical film work in the first year includes planning and scripting, scheduling, budgeting, camera and lighting, sound, editing and basic animation. Television work includes simple theory and broadcasting procedures, and practical production experience where each student is expected to operate in each branch of studio and control-room procedure. There are regular collaborations with schools of drama and music.

Second-year students are given a budget with which they can set up productions either in film or television, working with a staff producer. They are also encouraged to enter one or more of the seven departments of the school for specialist courses, and are obliged to undertake a major critical essay for the Department of General Studies, normally dealing with some aspect of history, aesthetics, philosophy or technique.

The third year is almost entirely devoted to practical pro-duction work. Students are again given a budget with which to set up a production which can be undertaken in co-operation with other students. For instance, a student majoring in camera may add his budget to that of a student majoring in direction or editing. Normally students will work on upwards of fifteen productions during their three years' study, although there is no definitive number of productions laid down. The intention is that they should gain a balanced experience in the whole range of production and develop one or more specializations.

The school has a strong tradition of documentary work, but productions also range from those dealing with science through to fiction and drama. It has long-established working links with the London Academy of Music and Dramatic Art and other schools of acting, the Royal College of Music and the Imperial College of Science and Technology. It is also used as a centre for lectures and film shows and has many links with learned and technical societies and the film and television in-dustries.

The complex pattern of post-graduate work makes it hard to summarize the course structure beyond saying that it is essentially practical and designed to meet the individual needs and aspirations of a wide variety of students, not only from the United Kingdom, but from many other countries throughout the world. The broad lines of the course develop from a strict technical introduction towards increasing creative freedom, so that in their last year students tend to work in a 'workshop' situation, using staff producers as consultants rather than teachers in the strict sense. Television and film for television are major activities in the school, and this side of its work is likely to increase with the newly equipped colour television studio. Short mid-career courses for television creative staff and technicians are actively being planned. These courses are intended not only for British students but also those from abroad, particularly small countries with no television training facilities.

The National Film School

This new school was opened in October 1971. Its facilities and course structure are being developed. Its director, Colin Young, formerly Chairman of the faculty of theatre arts in the University of California, Los Angeles, writes of his school:

> The National Film School has been established for professional training. Thus it is located unambiguously in an education context. It may be able to offer short courses for specialists in other fields, it may hope to upgrade the training of current professionals but its main task is to train a new generation of film-makers. It cannot at the same time accept the job of film study in a more general sense and diverts all inquiries about such work to the universities.
>
> Its curriculum is still being formed, as the first course starts in October 1971. The two main emphases will be upon film authorship (the individual stamp of the author) and on group work (the collaborative pooling of creative resources). This pairing itself represents the paradox of film work, and the attempt will be made to form students into small operating companies with a programme of films (and television productions) which will expand their abilities and require them to anticipate the requirements of professional work. As much as possible a line between training and professionalism must be drawn early in the course, so that as much time as possible is spent in a professional attitude. The teaching staff will be professionals so that their requirements to continue their own work must be met.
>
> Any training programme of this sort is an attempt to create a generation of artists. This one will be no different.

The school is sited some twenty-five miles out of central London at Beaconsfield.

It has recruited twenty-five students in its first year and

is likely to expand to a total of 100-120 students in a few years' time.

The London Film School (LFS) (formerly the London School of Film Technique)

This is a non-profit-making independent school which incorporates the long-established Overseas Film Training School. It is numerically the largest film school in the United Kingdom with a high proportion of overseas students. The Principal, Robert Dunbar, writes:

> We believe film-making to be an art in the sense that painting, music and poetry are arts. But, like architecture, film-making is also a technique and a business; like the theatre it is entertainment; like literature it is a means of communication.
>
> Although we do not set out to train actors as such, we have found that students need acting workshops and the like to prepare them for direction of all types of film—not only fiction.
>
> The two year Diploma Course in the arts and techniques of film-making is not patterned on other academic disciplines but is based on the practice and experience of professionals working in all branches of the film industry. Heads of department and course directors are all experienced film-makers and students are expected to conform to workshop disciplines.
>
> We believe narrow technical specialization to be a hindrance to the future of film-making—at the box office, as an art form and as a means of communication. We accept students as potential film-makers and not as 'editors', 'directors', 'cameramen' or 'scriptwriters'.
>
> Students begin to specialize in certain departments—especially during the second year of their studies—but they are better specialists for knowing something about the work of other departments, for knowing 'why' as well as 'how'.
>
> At the same time, our group system often produces highly integrated small units who have learnt to work together at the school, and continue to work together after they have left; such groups seem to be particularly viable in the present condition of the industry.

LFS—general aims and philosophy

The group system works democratically in that students form their own units and allocate jobs. Choice of subject and script is also made by the students—but the economic and practical framework is necessarily strict. We try to give the maximum of conceptual freedom within sets of physical conditions laid down for each film exercise.

Students must work on at least one film exercise each term, i.e. minimum of six during the course.

Some two years ago, we abolished written examinations and rely almost entirely on oral examinations conducted separately and individually by various heads of department. We have found this system not only more accurate but much more helpful to the students themselves.

The Polytechnic of Central London

The School of Film is part of the larger Department of Photography which has a high reputation for scientific and technical work.

Film is studied through all three years of the course, and is exclusively, either in theory or in practice, during years two and three.

The basic educational philosophy is to approach the study of film from five separate areas and to integrate these separate approaches into a unified whole. The course is based on five fundamental concepts:

To understand the film medium. a systematic knowledge of the principles of the photographic process and of sound recording is necessary.

A systematic knowledge of the relationship between image and word is also necessary.

Film is a part of man's culture. It is essential that its study is related to an appreciation of the arts in general, and in particular to the philosophy underlying the arts.

The study of the history of film permits a deeper understanding of the potentialities and limitations of the film medium; their relationships to technical change, social environment and financial control.

The successful practice of film production not only demands creative ability allied to a thorough knowledge of the film medium, but also demands organizational ability allied to administrative acumen.

The final year of the course culminates in the student being required to complete a film project, write a dissertation on an aesthetic aspect of film, and to demonstrate his ability to handle the business and administrative aspect of film production.

Outline of the course

The course is deliberately designed to give flexibility for individual development after the first year, which is diagnostic, and

Broadcast colour-television control room.
View from sound control room to director and gallery.
Royal College of Art,
School of Film and Television, London.

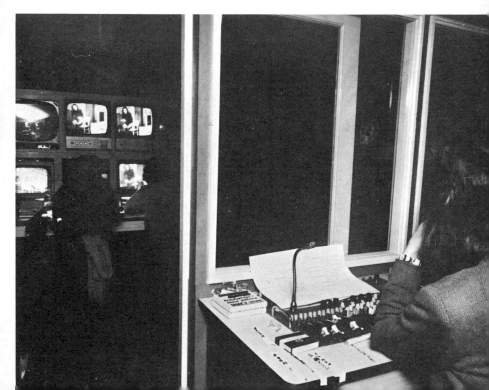

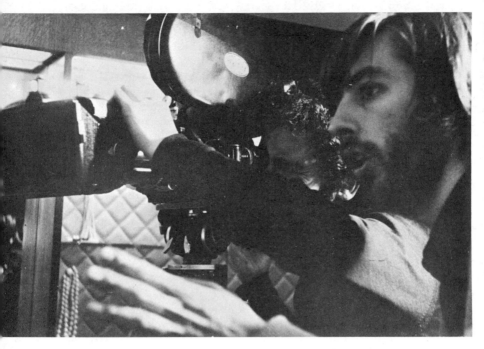

*16-mm filming on location. Royal College of Art,
School of Film and Television, London.*

a desirable proportion of time is given to tutorials, seminars and private study. Extracurricular study is encouraged and there are facilities for students in the evenings.

Subjects of the course

First year: the principles of the photographic process; aesthetics; design and visual studies; communication.

Second year: the principles of the photographic process (colour); design and visual studies; aesthetics; business organization; *and either:* option A—photography (applied photography; history of photography; printing and colour) *or* option B—film (film production; history of film; sound and television studies).

Third year: option A—photography (applied photography; aesthetics of photography; business management (photography)) *or* option B—film (film production; aesthetics of film; business organization (film and television)).

The project

During the third year each student is expected to complete a project, involving library research and some research into the agreed topic and either the taking of photographs or the making of a film, and including a written report. Projects will take the form of a professional commission or the exploration of visual concepts in a progressive manner.

The dissertation

Each student will be expected to complete a piece of written work, involving library search and research into an agreed topic based on aesthetics of either photography or film as appropriate to the option being studied (third year).

University of Bristol, Department of Drama: certificate in radio, film and television course

The one-year course is available to both graduates and undergraduates in radio, film and television. It is an introduction to the skills required in practical work in the three media.

The first term consists of a crash course of technical information to enable students to pursue a variety of practical projects in the remainder of the session.

The work includes making several films, both fictional and documentary; the recording of a radio play; and the preparation of videotape programmes. The film and television activities include both location and studio work.

Film training in the BBC

The BBC runs a number of training courses for both film and television. In the main they are concerned with vocational training for those already working in the corporation.

The BBC has a television training section instructing staff directors, production assistants, producer's assistants (i.e. production secretaries) and assistant film-makers in direction and production duties in television and film. The section is housed in its own building at Woodstock Grove, Shepherd's Bush, where it has a small studio, rehearsal rooms, production offices, lecture and projection rooms, cutting rooms, etc. The television studio is primarily for overseas training, which is housed in the same building, but is useful to BBC staff training at initial stages. At later stages courses move to service studios at Television Centre or Lime Grove Studios. Make-up training is also housed at Woodstock Grove. Film training is given in the Television training section at various different levels.

Television production courses

Basic professional training is given in the television training courses (two a year). These are twelve weeks long and the film training spreads over about five weeks of this. Courses consist of twelve directors, twelve producer's assistants, four production assistants and four assistant film-makers. The directors and production assistants get film training in three stages:

After instruction, each acts in turn as cameraman (with a Bolex) and director in turn, using course members as performers, in a simple and brief shooting exercise, edited by themselves.

Second, each directs a mute filmed exercise using other course members as actors, serviced by a professional camera crew and editors. Production assistants act as directors as well as doing their own production assistance job for the directors; producer's assistants also take part, shot listing, watching continuity, etc.

Third, a final exercise working with a professional sync camera crew, with a budget allocation enabling artists or other professional performers to be engaged. The film subject is director's own choice; production assistants aid them as do producer's assistants with the scripting, scheduling, shot listing, etc. Editing is professionally done as is the dubbing. The films are analysed in group sessions. The emphasis of the training is on preparation, efficient use of time and resources and low shooting ratios, plus how a director works efficiently with professional crews.

Advanced film courses

Two per year for twelve directors and four producer's assistants, all of whom have already done some filming for their departments, know some of the problems and now require advanced training.

This is a five-week course, basically workshop, with a number of skilled directors from the BBC and outside coming in to talk about the director's job with film clips. A number of different filming exercises take place ranging from do-it-yourself filming and editing to going on the sound stage at Ealing Film Studios with a full scale set and all the complications of lighting, large film crew, artists, make-up, etc.

The last two and a half weeks are spent in preparing final exercises; shooting them with a professional synchronizing crew, artists, etc., as needed (a budget is provided); professional editing and dubbing with final analyses conducted in a group session.

Films are shown, dissected and discussed to understand directing techniques.

The aim is to help young directors to become proficient technically and artistically, to work with professionals in the United Kingdom and abroad, and to gain maximum impact with minimum expenditure of time, footage and money.

There are also courses for the news films, producer's assistants and for overseas students, but these are outside the true scope of this report and therefore are not dealt with in any detail.

Film training—general approach and philosophy

Hannen Foss, Head of Film Training, BBC, writes:

1. We are training professionals to take a skilled part in a complex and difficult medium, television.
2. Directors have to work all the time through other professionals (cameramen, sound recordists, editors, etc.) and must have skill in getting the best out of these men and recognizing the strong union involvement in the job being done, i.e. they must learn to take their place in a tightly structured, strictly unionized industry and still be creative.
3. Teaching of film directing can only be done (if it can be done!) by: (a) looking at the best work done in film; (b) knowing how directors have achieved their results; (c) a full knowledge of technical possibilities and limitations.

The aim of training is:

1. To initiate young directors into a *professional* outlook about film. They must know film grammar, responsibilities, skills, and how to work with other professionals, artists, cameramen, editors, musicians, writers, etc.
2. To show economies may be made in filming, non-sequential shooting, pre-planning, preparation methods, passing out information to others working with you so there is a maximum team effort and comprehension when the expensive job of filming starts. Low shooting ratios are stressed.
3. How to work at speed and yet maintain high professional standards. This is highly relevant in television filming; it may also be relevant to theatrical filming since high costs and extravagances are making less risk capital available for film-making. Directors who show they can work skilfully and fast may restore financial confidence for film-making.
4. People can be shown good examples, given good precepts by good practitioners, but finally they have to find out for themselves. The practical is therefore ultimately the learning medium.

I like to give instruction or advice before practical, requesting that certain issues be tackled in the practical (e.g. first shooting may be to get good shots which cut together; second may concentrate on working with a pro crew, words of control, directing artists etc.). Then analysis of the practical in group session focuses good and bad points from each film so that all can learn from it.

The chief aim is to get trainee directors to prepare realistically and use time well when shooting. I assume they have visual talent and abundant ideas—it isn't my job to instruct them in these. My role is to teach them to operate in a professional way. Whether they are gifted or not will be decided by the films they make and the opinion of their departments.

Finally, I probably have an advantage over film schools, whose function seems to me unclearly defined, in that course members are already in television. This urges them to be a bit more serious and ready to learn because they are in a very competitive field and know their work will be compared with the best being done.

Smaller production schools

In addition to the major schools there are many film and television departments in schools and colleges at every level. The most significant of these are to be found in the polytechnics, technical colleges and colleges of art and design. In the main they fall into three groups: first, approaching the subject from a strongly technical and scientific basis; second, as an art form, particularly as an extension of the visual arts and, third, as a general subject extending a liberal studies course. The schools vary widely in size, equipment and levels of professionalism. They serve film and television in the broadest sense and more particularly they provide a limited number of recruits for the lower grades of technical employment, and are one of the main sources of recruitment for the larger professional schools.

Among these schools the most important are to be found in the colleges of art in Bournemouth, Portsmouth, London, Hornsey, Ravensbourne (chiefly concerned with television techniques), the Technical College, Harrow, the London College of Printing, and the polytechnics of Leeds, Birmingham and Wolverhampton. There are also a large number of small departments scattered throughout the country which tend to provide equipment, and encouragement rather than regular courses at a professional level.

The proliferation of these schools is an indication of the growing acceptance that the making of film and television is a part of our normal social and cultural environment, and as such should be given increasing educational support.

It is also of interest to note that there are two well-established educational television training courses for foreign students run by the Centre for Educational Development Overseas, based in London, and by Thompson College in Glasgow. They normally run short intensive production courses.

Supporting institutions and associations

Film and television culture in the United Kingdom and the educational provision made to support it should not be seen simply as being limited to the practice of film and television production. The study of the history, aesthetics and social context of these subjects is of great significance, not only for the general public but also for the directors and other creative artists working professionally. This latter influence expresses itself in two ways; first, in the direct effect it has on the creative film- and television-director in deepening his awareness of the full range of his calling and, second, in helping to educate a responsive and informed audience, thus encouraging a wider and deeper use of the twin media.

By far and away the most important single organization in this group is the British Film Institute. Its Director, Stanley Reed, writing especially for this report, describes its broad educational role:[1]

1. In May 1972, Keith Lucas was named Director of the British Film Institute.

The British Film Institute was founded to 'encourage the development of the art of the film, to promote its use as a record of contemporary life and manners, and to foster public appreciation and study of it'. The institute does have a similar responsibility for television. The institute consists of the National Film Archive, the National Film Theatre—and in addition forty regional film theatres—the Education Department, film distribution, publications and production board.

The institute is, of course, a wholly educational body in the broad sense; our central purpose is public education. But the institute also has two more specifically educational tasks within the structure of formal education, and has established an Education Department with particular responsibility for these.

The first of these two tasks is to establish the study of film within education, at all levels from primary school to university. The serious study of film in this country (as in most others) is still at a very rudimentary stage. The aesthetics of film are scarcely explored and even the factual history of the cinema is inadequately documented and assessed.

Because the universities have not yet got to grips with these tasks, the British Film Institute is to some extent looked to, through its publications, the programme selections of the National Film Theatre, and its Education Department, as the fount of wisdom on these matters. But the institute is not a competent or proper body to undertake these tasks: as a centralized and State-supported body, we must, and do, repudiate this task. On the other hand, it is certainly our job to persuade universities and other academics to assume these tasks.

At other levels of education proper forms of film study should also be established. Thus we believe that every child should have some education in moving pictures as they have in the spoken and written word.

The best service the institute can perform is to provide practical services for lecturers and teachers working in the field. They need films and film extracts, and information about films. These we try to provide through our film library, our publications and our information services.

The second area of education in which we engage is that of film use for teaching purposes. We are not concerned with conventional 'visual aids' particularly at school level, but rather with the selection and use of material in general distribution. This may come from the film archives of the world, from television, or from feature and documentary films.

Film Institute
production board

The production board is intended to serve a double role: (a) to seek out completely new and untried talent and (b) to help those who have proven their abilities to take the difficult next step into commercial feature production. In this latter task particularly, the institute would hope to keep in close touch with the film schools.

There are also two University Departments specializing in the study of film history. They are the Film Department in the Slade School of Fine Art, in the University of London, and the American Arts Documentation Centre in the University of Exeter.

Professor Thorold Dickinson, who recently retired from the Slade School writes:

> The job of the university is to prepare people either to be active in film promotion or in teaching and criticism, or to be a discriminating leaven in the audience, to nose out the promising and the good, to keep the passive audience from relapsing into acceptance of the commonplace, the mere-tricious and the phoney, which even they sooner or later will find themselves no longer bothering to support. There are also a small number of students of production who find the freer atmosphere of the university more stimulating than the intensive practicalities of the training school.
>
> At the Slade School in University College London, the backbone of the study is bombardment by film three times a week, with programmes co-ordinated to give in two years a survey of the development of the medium in many countries. There are weekly group seminars for full-time post-graduate students. The nature of the programmes is based on my own conviction that over its first seventy-five years of existence cinema has been changing, hope-fully developing, and will continue to do so to a marked degree, influenced by current events which change the attitudes of film-makers and promoters, and their audience, and that success derives from the makers and the audience keeping in step and hence in harmony.
>
> The Slade is trying to develop one obvious educational asset of cinema: the visual and audible records of historical evidence. We have a four-year contract with the Social Science Research Council building up a national catalogue of film existent in Britain of historical significance, the first such register in any nation, we believe.
>
> For the past few years the Slade has been operating a modest co-operative scheme, known as UCOLFILM and backed by a revolving fund from the Calouste Gulbenkian Foundation, by which centres of higher education sub-

scribe to the ownership of films, grouped under subjects, which are otherwise unavailable in Britain.

The scope for the film in the university ranges from the aesthetic study of cinema through its historical and sociological contacts to its utility as a means of educational communication. We also try to vitalize theoretical work with a measure of practical performance by staff and students.

Dr Michael Weaver describes the work in the American Arts Sub-department in the Department of English at the University of Exeter:

Undergraduate study of the American film is taught within the two-year American Arts course in Britain. This important field tends to be neglected in university film scholarship and criticism, and film production courses, placing the emphasis on creativity, do very little to promote serious film study.

The Exeter film study course takes an author approach, and each student studies two major authors (e.g. Griffith, Ford, Lang, Welles, Flaherty) exhaustively over a three-month period (complete works of these authors where possible—up to sixteen films by Ford and Lang, for instance). Aspects of four more authors of a lesser stature (e.g. Peckinpah, Fleischer, Anger, Lorentz, von Sternberg, Penn, etc.) are also studied. This work, spread over two years, produces essays of a quality equal to the best undergraduate essays on literature, drama or art. Although based on the American cinema, international relationships are also studied. Thus, the whole of Lang's work is studied, both German and American, and when Renoir is studied his French work will be included. American cinema is still the major national cinema in the world, and one of its strengths as a focus for a film study course is the wealth of international talent it has attracted. Research for a Ph.D. on the influence of German Expressionism on the American film is well advanced, and study for an M.A. on Fritz Lang's American films has just begun. There is a strong demand for opportunities for film research at university level.

There are also many societies who attempt to encourage and disseminate film and television studies. The Society for Education in Film and Television is particularly concerned with the film and television education of the young. The Federation of British Film Societies, with over 700 member clubs, encourages both film-viewing and film-making in the age group of 16 years and over, and serves a very wide public both inside and outside the educational world. The British Film Academy and the Society for Film and Television Arts are associations of professionals who meet to view, discuss and encourage the making of film and television. The Royal Television Society and the British Kinematograph, Sound and Television Society are essentially concerned with the encouragement of craft and technology, and act to some extent as a continuing mid-career educational force.

The attitude of the major trade union in the film and television industry, the Association of Film and Television Technicians (ACTT), is also important since its views have been considered influential, particularly in the setting up of the National Film School. Alan Sapper, the General Secretary, describes the ACTT's attitude to film education:

> There should be established a comprehensive vocational film training scheme run by the Department of Education and Science which would receive young entrants to the industry and train them to a proficiency to enable their participation in the professional film production field commencing at junior posts. It would therefore be necessary for secondary modern and comprehensive schools to utilize such a vocational training scheme as their degree or certification courses. Entry to such a vocational training scheme should not be dependent on academic qualifications.
>
> The training scheme should also supply the facilities for re-training persons unemployed owing to changing technology so that they can usefully earn a living in the allied fields of film-making. There should be no limitation academically or agewise placed upon entry into this stream. The training scheme should be allied to other training schemes and boards so as the transference from one industry to other industries can be facilitated. Also, there should be courses covering all grades so that, for instance, an unemployed cameraman can re-train for air control operational duties at an airport or a scene painter can re-train for textile design, etc.
>
> Before such a vocational training scheme can be established agreement must be obtained with employer and Government bodies for: (a) guaranteed employment at the end of the schemes' courses and; (b) that a real living wage, probably three times that which is paid at the present training board courses, should be made available to men and women in the course of re-training.
>
> The fundamental principle of such a scheme should be training personnel not only for a specific new job but to give them a theoretical base so that any further developments in technology would not mean them having to go through a completely new course from fundamentals onwards again. As a first step to obtain such a scheme there should be a rationalization of the present film training facilities and their being urgently linked to training boards and employers' organizations as described above.

Conclusions

The diverse educational opportunities for the creative film- or television-director in the United Kingdom in the early 1970s are beginning to shape themselves into a recognizable and adequate provision, although there are still many deficiencies, particularly in the encouragement of film and television history and aesthetics. The British Film Institute has grown enormously during the last decade, and its work has gained in importance and influence. Although it still has need of continuing and developing support the institute is a uniquely important force in the United Kingdom.

The film and television societies and professional associations grouped together provide a substantial potential for mid-career support. The production schools, after a slow start (our National Film School was founded nearly fifty years after that in the U.S.S.R.) are at last beginning to provide the necessary range of opportunities, although it is important to realize that they do not work on the same basis as many of the major schools in Eastern Europe. Less importance is given to 'dramaturgy' as such, and direction and script-writing are encouraged to develop out of a wide basis of production experience, rather than being treated as separate subjects in isolation. Schools of acting have been slow to see the importance of combining their work with that of the schools of film and television, and this has delayed the development of direct training for entry into the feature film industry. This has remained an area of education handicapped by stubborn indifference, encouraged by the sharp reduction of feature film production during the last decade. As has been pointed out earlier in this report, entry into the shrinking feature film industry is commonly made via television and film-making for television, which serves as a useful proving ground for this crucial area of work. At least one school, that in the Royal College of Art, traditionally trains its graduates for both electronic and filmed television and in this sense is well suited to the particular needs of this country. In the author's view it is too early to see how the new National Film School will alter the present balance of film education but it seems possible, and indeed sensible if it seeks to develop the areas of film-making least fully provided for in the present educational structure. The Royal College of Art should develop its truly post-graduate work as an international centre for electronic television and film for television.

George Stevens Jr

United States of America

Film-making is coming to be recognized as the most complex of all the arts requiring, in its great practitioners, in addition to a grasp of many individual arts, crafts, and technologies, a humanistic outlook and philosophical background, qualities of leadership, and courage. Moreover, as cinema has existed for less than a century, it is short on theory, and the education of the film-maker is one of the least well defined of all educational processes.

The film-maker is defined in this chapter as the person centrally responsible for making a film; he may be the director, writer, producer, or a combination of all three; the word film is used to cover feature pictures, documentaries, television, and abstract or experimental work. All the references relate to film-making in the United States, and in particular to the learning of the creative process (on the assumption—which may not always be true—that the film-maker gains his humanistic and philosophical education elsewhere).

History and origins

Simply making films has been the traditional basis for learning how to make films in the United States, starting from the early part of this century and the first films made by Edwin S. Porter (*The Great Train Robbery*) and later pioneers like D. W. Griffith and Chaplin. The quality of these early films and the powers of invention and imagination of their makers are miraculous when one considers that they were the beginners. There was very little left to invent by the time D. W. Griffith had made his masterpieces. From then on, it was largely a question of refining film language. This was done by succeeding generations of film-makers in association with accomplished craftsmen, many of whom came from Europe and from the theatre.

The film industry was soon producing thousands upon thousands of films, and providing the greatest training ground the medium would probably ever know; its concentration in southern California encouraged a synergistic exchange of knowledge and talent. This very advantage was later to become a drawback. As time passed, Hollywood became increasingly powerful and jealous of its power, turned protectionist, making its studios almost impenetrable and increasingly less welcoming to newcomers.

This rigidity was generalized after the Second World War. To its later regret, the industry at first ignored a new medium and competition, television, whose capture of a mass audience started the decline of the companies which had dominated the international film scene for three decades.

By the 1950s, very little education was being provided within the industry, since the decline in production had led to a decline in the opportunities open to new people. The few film schools in universities had had no impact whatsoever.

During the 1950s and 1960s technological innovation in the form of portable sound cameras and high-speed film took film-making outside the studio walls, and put it into the hands of new kinds of people. Film was beginning at long last to be taken seriously by cultural and academic leaders who had hitherto looked upon film as frivolous and low class, and rarely as a creative art form and communications force. The resulting film explosion, like most occasions of great or rapid change, had its beneficial and its negative sides.

Film was at last taken seriously by the academic world which, gradually and uncertainly, began to open its gates to film studies. New opportunities appeared for young people who had previously been virtually excluded from responsible roles in film production.

Some of them, however, did not fully appreciate the discipline and knowledge required to ensure a successful film career. Robert Steele, a professor at Boston University, said that:

> Many of them are not well read enough to be English majors and others do not want to spend the time studying in a scientific course. Film looks like an easy thing, and I am sure that lethargy and indolence brings a lot of them into film-making.

Staff of the Department of Photography and Cinema
discussing a story-board for a production.
[Photo: Ohio State University.]

Staff members and student checking a student-staff production on the Steenbeck editing bench.
[Photo: Ohio State University.]

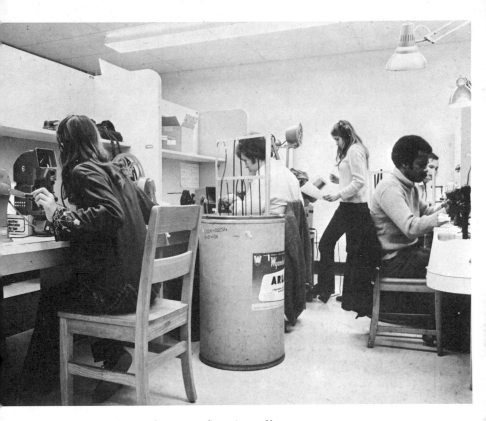

Student editing of 16-mm or Super-8-mm film.
[Photo: Ohio State University.]

In an era which advocated letting the young 'do their own thing' it was forgotten that, as in any art form, there is a great deal in cinema also which should be learned methodically.

Previously they had been excluded because they were young, now they were sought out because they were young. Sadly, they were for the most part unprepared for the opportunities thrust upon them, and the industry's preoccupation with youth was short lived.

Film schools in the 1970s

Almost all formal education of film-makers takes place in universities in the United States; there is no equivalent of the national academies which exist in Europe. (The Center for Advanced Film Studies, a 'conservatory' established by the American Film Institute in 1968, is one exception, and is discussed separately below.) In 1971 the institute made a survey of courses in 427 colleges and universities which either teach film-making or enable students to study film as art. In 1971 over 3,000 students were studying film-making in ninety-six universities. Three-fourths were undergraduates simultaneously doing a general university education. Most intend to make a career in film-making, but experience indicates that many will change their minds. At forty-seven of these universities, degrees in film-making are awarded, and the percentage of their graduates who continue to a film-making career is higher, but many who have advanced degrees seem to drift to other callings because of lack of opportunity, a change of interest, or the belated discovery of the difficulty of becoming a successful film-maker.

Two developments may be mentioned at this point.

First, film is being introduced into interdisciplinary courses which also include anthropology, history, and the social or political sciences; in some cases, several universities run a joint course on these lines.

Second, secondary-school teachers are being trained to teach film as art or as a medium of communication. Inundated by television and other visual media, the secondary schools are beginning to recognize an obligation to teach young people to discriminate between programmes of value and the others. However, teachers (especially those whose training was literary) are still often hesitant about the idea of film as a classroom subject. The late George Amberg of New York University held the view that 'there should be professional schools for film-makers. An artist should not have to fill academic requirements. And the university should not give degrees for non-academic work.'

In all, some 6,000 students are studying film in universities throughout the country. In addition to the 427 which
have at least one film course and the 100 which offer a comprehensive course in film, almost every important university is
considering the incorporation of visual media studies into its
curricula.

A new survey updating the 1971 inquiry made by the
American Film Institute and including television for the first
time[1] gives detailed information on film and television courses
in 613 American colleges, including course titles, names of
faculty, and the type of equipment available for students.

The University of Southern California (USC) has the
longest continuing university film course, dating back to 1929
when it offered an introduction to the photoplay. By 1971 its
Cinema Department had grown to the extent of offering four
different academic degrees, some seventy-five courses, and employing twenty-four full-time and eighteen part-time professors.
Guest lecturers have included Jerry Lewis and George Cukor.
There are 100 undergraduates and 350 graduate students. Graduates are noted for their technical proficiency, and USC is generally thought of as being very much commercially aware in its
film training courses.

The University of California at Los Angeles (UCLA), on
the opposite side of Los Angeles from USC, takes a more indi-
vidualistic approach. Students rotate roles on production crews
in USC; in UCLA, each is encouraged to make his own film as
a personal statement. It is one of the best equipped universities,
and estimates that half of its film graduates have found work
in some aspect of commercial, educational or documentary
film-making. Francis Ford Coppola studied at UCLA and is
now an established director. George Lucas graduated from USC
and, under the umbrella of Coppola's production company,
made a feature film for Warner Brothers which was an expansion of his thesis film at USC, *THX 1138*.

These are but two out of the forty-three universities in
the state of California alone which offer courses in cinema.

New York University (NYU) and Columbia University
are among the leaders on the east coast. Several years ago NYU
established an ambitious Institute of Film and Television under
the direction of producer Robert Saudek, but it lasted only a
year because of conflicts within the university and dissatisfaction
among the students. It has recently been revived and represents
one of three segments of NYU's film activities. The others are
the undergraduate programme for 400 students, and a pro-

1. *The American Film Institute Guide to College Courses in Film
and Television*, Acropolis Books, 1973.

Film sound equipment.
[Photo: Ohio State University.]

The advanced direction course begins
with videotape sketches of the action and ends
with the shooting of a film based on a script selected
from a previous seminar on screenplay writing.
[Photo: Ohio State University.]

*Social science research using pictorial rather
than verbal techniques.*
[Photo: Ohio State University.]

gramme (fifty-five graduate students) in which film is studied as a 'humanist discipline'. Documentary film-maker Arthur Barron restructured the Columbia film training programme, which is for graduate students only. The School of Visual Arts also in New York leans towards the professional school approach and is non-university.

Temple University in Pennsylvania offers 'film as creative documentary, cinema vérité, film as anthropological statement, and film as journalism'. The San Francisco state programme lays the emphasis on experimental film-making. Nearby Stanford University in Palo Alto concentrates wholly on documentary with graduate students. Stanford is one of the most respected private universities in the United States, and its Film Department has a teaching relationship with the Canadian Film Board.

The University of Iowa, Michigan University, Ohio State University, Ohio University and Northwestern University all offer film courses. In fact, the University of Iowa had the first in the country, in 1916, and is now famous for creative film-writing courses. The University of Texas could prove an excellent centre for regional university film-making in an area where there is considerable wealth and industry.

Several of the Ivy League universities in New England have film programmes. These vary widely. At Harvard, film comes under 'visual and environmental studies'. The Massachusetts Institute of Technology brought in the well-known maker of documentaries, Richard Leacock, for a teaching, research and development programme of work on 8-mm synchronous sound in conjunction with its own scientists. This collaboration of artist and scientists could have interesting results. Boston University and Yale each offer film courses. Yale has the additional advantage of being able to draw upon its excellent school of theatre arts.

These various universities are among the most prominent, but are a mere sample of the cinema studies available in universities in the United States.

University studies today

Academic study in other arts dates back hundreds, and in some cases, thousands of years, whereas film came upon the world scene less than a century ago and has had only a few decades to establish its standing. However, it can be only a matter of time in the United States until a full awareness of the significance of film as a social force ensures resources for film study that are proportionate to its importance and take due account of its unavoidably high costs.

Aside from financial considerations, a basic difficulty is that universities have simultaneously to teach a complex art and provide a full education. One or other usually suffers. Frequently a student acquires only a little know-how about several aspects of film-making and even less of the essentials of a proper education. Some universities have adopted the solution of allowing students to begin cinema studies only after graduating. This is useful provided that gifted graduates can join a superior graduate school of cinema whose staff and resources are on a par with those of the finest schools of architecture or medicine.

People qualified to teach film-making in universities are scarce. Experts can be found in the various technical crafts but few are qualified to lead students through the whole process, from script-writing to production, including directing actors, cinematography and design, film editing, and sound and music.

One professor is quoted as saying that he 'doesn't advise artistically, just technically'. This attitude is widespread. Very often the instructor is simply not qualified to do any more, particularly if he has become a teacher directly, without acquiring practical experience in the cinema. Much of the learning in universities is confined to acquiring a technical understanding; the rest is based on the 'learn by doing' principle. This was effective in the industry in its heyday, but it is not nowadays on a basis of collaborating with amateurs on a few small films over a two or three year period. A dogmatic or narrow approach in film-teaching could be disastrous, but certain principles of film-making can certainly be imparted by accomplished professionals serving as tutors.

The limited ability of instructors is both the cause and the effect of short-comings in university training. There is also a dearth of teaching materials. The shortage of qualified tutors would be less crippling if the university library had books that could fill the gaps or copies of the great film works of the past that could easily be consulted. Most of the books available in English are almost wholly concerned with film history, criticism and 'scholarship', with next to nothing on the creative aspects (especially first-hand accounts from film-makers themselves). Film people are seldom literary and usually do not write about their art; moreover, the universities ignored film for many years, and did nothing to finance or encourage this type of writing. They could now make amends and help to finance the production of films and books about film-making, and a programme of international translations of existing books on film theory and film-making (in which Unesco might also take a leading role).

The American Film Institute's Center for Advanced Film Studies is recording dialogues with experienced film-makers

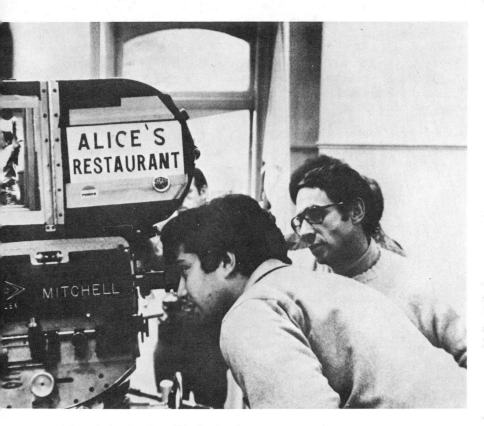

*Through the American Film Institute's
internship programme, funded by the Academy
of Motion Picture Arts and Sciences,
Jeff Young was able to study film production first-hand
with Arthur Penn during the filming of* Alice's Restaurant.

which will gradually be made available in print, on audio tape, and on film. An hour and a half feature length film on the work of John Ford, written and directed by Peter Bogdanovich, is one example.

I have not dealt with curricula because of the sheer numbers of universities involved and also because I believe that curricula problems will be considerably reduced when teaching materials of the kind just described become generally available.

Equipment problems can be readily solved if the funds are provided. Universities have in fact allocated funds more readily for the purchase of equipment than for the preparation of teaching materials and the employment of expert staff—no doubt because physical problems are easier to deal with than intellectual and artistic.

Despite all these difficulties, I find the outlook optimistic. Inertia has disappeared, and academic interest in film has acquired variety and quality. Hundreds of universities will contribute skill and talent from both their teaching staffs and from their students. As the film industry ceases to be monolithic, the universities can assume a greater role in film-making in the different parts of the country and increasingly attract talented staff.

A catalytic role in this respect can be played by the Center for Advance Film Studies, which is described in the next section.

A national conservatory

The American Film Institute was set up in 1967 by the federal government, following a survey (commissioned by the National Endowment for the Arts) made by the Stanford Research Institute to determine the structure and functions of the proposed institute. One conclusion was that:

> The training of the artists who create film is perhaps the most important single function which a national film institution could undertake . . . there is no other function that can have so direct a bearing on the state of the art or so immediate effect on the quality of the art.

Two other conclusions relate to the Center for Advanced Film Studies:

> . . . a significant gap in the total professional development system appears to exist between the formal education system (i.e. university film schools) and professional experience.
>
> . . . except for a few notable exceptions, the faculties and staffs of U.S. film schools seldom include a significant number of successful film artists.

*A graduate makes his first feature film
at the American Film Institute Centre.*

The centre was to provide a bridge between the film schools and the professional film-makers and it sought to attract talented professionals into the educational process. A rent-free mansion made available by the city of Beverly Hills is close to the film-making community in Los Angeles, where hundreds of artists and craftsmen reside. The centre became a kind of conservatory in which young people were accepted for individual education. Each candidate (a) is accepted after his or her basic education; (b) is expected to have previously acquired basic skills in cinema or be accomplished in another artistic medium; (c) must have decided upon a career in film-making.

The centre accepted its first students in the autumn of 1969, and the first two years were for all of us staff and students alike an intensive period of learning. Our aim was to provide a structure in which talented young people could learn under individual guidance and define and expand their own talents. The curriculum included film screenings, seminars with professional film-makers, and production of films with tutorial guidance from professional advisers and staff from the centre.

The centre opened during the film explosion of the sixties referred to earlier, and this contributed to its growing pains. Having selected from 300 applicants the twenty presumed to be the most talented, we created a situation, as we discovered later, which made learning very difficult. The first entrants were justly proud to have been chosen, but some apparently soon began to consider that learning was secondary and that the centre existed simply to provide resources and equipment for film-making. After a year and a half, one however said: 'Just now am I beginning to realise how much there is to learn. I wish I could start over.'

After the experience of the first year we began to revise procedures at the centre. Attendance at seminars and screenings had at first been voluntary, on the assumption that these very advanced young professionals could decide for themselves how best to allocate their time. In accepting the 1971 intake, we established different conditions and a different climate. All meetings and screenings during the first three months are now obligatory, and this period is used on both sides to decide whether or not to continue into the next phase, in which the student will produce his own films. This arrangement has attracted a more serious type of student, who knows in advance that the conservatory involves artistic discipline as well as specific learning.

Twenty are accepted each year for a two-year course, making a total at the centre of between fifty and sixty. The initial three-month period is devoted to seminars, script-writing, and small productions in teams of five which help to reveal to

*Bill Wilder (shown here with Center fellows) attends
a Fellini seminar at the American Film Institute's Center
for Advanced Film Studies.*

them and to us their strengths and weaknesses. In the next phase they embark on their own productions, sometimes also taking part in professional productions.

There are no examinations or grades. Each is helped to discover the gaps in his skills and seeks to fill them. The emphasis is to learn as much as possible by actual film-making. The purpose is to make film-makers, not films.

Learning is organized into five overlapping sectors: scriptwriting; directing actors; photography and production design; editing; and sound and music. These are explored in the screening and analysis of a diverse selection of films. Film analysis is at the heart of the learning process and is led by three permanent staff (Frantisek Daniel, dean of the centre; Antonio Vellani, vice-dean of the centre; and Jim Silke, chairman of film studios) who are joined by professional writers and directors in working with students on their screen-plays. There are seminars once or twice a week with guests who include noted directors (Fellini, Hitchcock, Hawks, Renoir) and writers, set designers, cameramen, editors, musicians, special effects experts—in fact the entire range of the arts and crafts involved. Regular acting classes fill a gap in the experience of many of the students and bring them into contact with professional players who may agree to appear in their films.

Individual progress has been quite remarkable, both in terms of the film work being done and the speed with which skills improve.

Expanding influence

The purpose of the centre is not only to train individuals but to provide an inspiration for film education throughout the United States. This is admittedly ambitious but our hopes are beginning to seem justified. The discussions which take place with the film professionals are published in a series called 'Dialogue on Film' which are sent to all film schools in the country. This series is gradually building up into an encyclopaedia based on the first-hand experiences and the insights of the world's leading film-makers. At the same time, the centre is inducing many of these professionals to consider the possibility of extending their careers to include teaching and tutoring; this may eventually recruit some of the accomplished artists whose absence probably constitutes the major deficiency of the university film schools.

A new programme will enable instructors from the university film schools to attend the centre for one month each year, to exchange information and views, and make contact with the professionals who come to the centre, and perhaps invite them to collaborate in their own schools.

The centre for Advanced Film Studies can be one part of a chain linking film education in the United States with the film industry, and putting a generation of young people who wish to express themselves through a career in film in touch with the world of art and industry which they seek to join and change.

Momčilo Ilić

Yugoslavia

However careful and successful, a study—and conclusions—limited to observation of the education of the film-maker in different countries risks being of very limited interest unless account is also taken of the future possibilities of development.

Our main purpose should therefore be to answer the question: for what kind of cinema and television are we to train key personnel?

This is the vital question, for it is increasingly evident that film-making is today at a turning point, mainly because of changes brought about by the technological revolution in various domains, and particularly in audio-visual communications.

We could frankly say that the major problem is no longer in exchanging teaching experiences between film schools, or in what the less developed can borrow from the more advanced. A common problem everywhere, even in countries which do not yet make films, is to foresee what new directions cinema will take. But the experience of some schools might serve to help others to get more quickly through certain phases of development. In that sense an account of the Yugoslav experience may perhaps be helpful.

It seems to us essential that film schools should keep ahead of progress. They can not do this by State decree, but rather by foreseeing in good time how cinema is developing—sooner and more clearly if possible than the cinema itself. Instead of waiting, even begging, for help and trying incessantly to prove they are necessary, the situation could change radically in the opposite direction: it is cinema and television that would have to ask the schools for help. That could be the great chance and they should be ready for it. This will be the main theme of this chapter, which is in two parts: past and present, and the future.

Past and present

The relatively long period between Lumière and the Second World War was the golden age of film-making in some countries. In Yugoslavia, it was a period of effort for a few ardent pioneers, and for some spontaneously-formed groups and organizations. Their work composed a precious chapter in Yugoslav film history.

Several hundred shorts of various kinds were made, and a dozen full-length films. The first news films of Belgrade were made in 1897, and the first full-length film was shot there in 1911. A brave attempt to start a film school in Zagreb in 1917 was repeated several times in the following years in Belgrade and in Zagreb. Film criticism appeared for the first time in 1920. But 1945 can be considered as the real first year of professional and organized film production in Yugoslavia, recognized and supported by the State and by society.

From the outset, technicians were a problem. Yugoslavia had practically none, and had to fall back on a few pre-war pioneers, mostly cameramen, and the do-it-yourself training picked up by those (the majority of them young) who took up cinema after the war and usually learned simply by making their own films.

The need for a more systematic education was obvious from the beginning. An Advanced School for Acting and Film Production, with a camera section, was opened in Belgrade in 1947, and new technical schools in Belgrade and Zagreb at secondary level trained sound engineers, lighting experts, cameramen, and other professionals.

The idea was good, but the difficulties (especially in dealing with technicians doing creative jobs) were almost insurmountable. The teachers knew little more than the students. More could hardly be expected than the six shorts produced in 1945 and the thirty-three in 1946. Full-length films began in 1947: two in that year, four in 1948, three in 1949.

Conditions at the time made it impossible to improve teaching at the Belgrade school, or invite better qualified staff from other countries.

In 1950 the school ceased to exist as such. For a time it

continued as a cinema section of the Theatrical Art Academy in Belgrade. It ceased completely in 1952–53, leaving little trace in the history of Yugoslav film-making.

The training problem remained open for years. Apart from a few who trained abroad, the creators learned by empirical film-making, sometimes doing expensive films.

After more than ten years of professional film-making, the general opinion was that if Yugoslav films did not come up to expectations, it was principally because there were not enough people who were properly trained and experienced.

The solution seemed to be to provide systematic education and training for those who already had practical professional or amateur experience, and so raise the average level of quite a number of people in a relatively short time.

Cinema Education Centre

The Cinema Education Centre (later called the Film Institute) was set up in 1961, with headquarters in Belgrade and a branch in Zagreb. Teaching was organized as follows (the duration being four semesters):

Admission

The minimum admission requirement was the secondary-school certificate (some students had university degrees). Some who came directly from film production had scholarships from the Serbian Cultural Council.

Syllabus

First semester. Social science principles; history of world cinema; history of the documentary; film aesthetics and means of expression; figurative arts; history of music; world literature; national literature; theatrical literature; basic technology of film-making.

Second semester. Practical work, the results to be submitted before the third semester. The candidate must make a short or study a problem, for example role and importance of the training film in the army, use of film in scientific research, role and importance of the assistant director in a documentary, drama and its development to date in Yugoslav film.

Each student could choose a tutor among the teaching staff or the outside specialists.

Third semester. Directing; theory of film drama; analysis of paintings; theory of perspective and space; shooting; special effects; laboratory procedures; sound recording; basic film editing; music in film; make-up; costume.

Fourth semester. Thesis, written examination, practicals.

Teaching employed audio-visual methods wherever possible, for example 948 slides were prepared for the history of world art course, and literature was taught by showing how to adapt books for the cinema.

The most successful course was the history of world film-making, thanks to possibilities which few film schools could equal—the Yugoslav film library was rich enough to allow this course to be given entirely in the form of screenings (seventy-seven complete films, and ninety-four excerpts of major world films), with analyses and commentary by the staff.

Another feature of the course was the attempt to investigate the relations between the art image and the film image by studying and analysing paintings.

The Zagreb course also included drawing for cartoon films.

The centre had separate sections for direction (including montage); set design; camera; production management. As a general rule, all students, regardless of their specialization, were required to take all subjects.

Teaching staff

The centre succeeded in recruiting to the staff people prominent in film in Yugoslavia (artists, professors, even members of the academy) and various eminent foreign directors (including Grierson, Cuhraj, Eisner, Jean Mitry, Bahman, Jean Painlevé); there were also a few technical assistance experts.

Each was usually asked to prepare a mimeographed out-one of his course; the twenty or so courses thus provided were lif great help to the students.

The problem of finding young technicians at university level began to be solved in the existing art academies (Belgrade, Ljubljana and Zagreb).

Academy of Theatre, Cinema, Radio and Television, Belgrade

The Academy of Theatrical Art, part of the Fine Arts Academy of Belgrade University, became the Academy of Theatre, Cinema, Radio and Television in 1963.

Its curricula have altered over the years. It was originally considered that theatre, film, radio and television all constituted representational art, and that students should acquire a knowledge of all four which would later allow them to work in whichever one they preferred—or in all of them.

In recent years, however, theatre and film have become separate sections, but share certain subject-matter.

The academy is organized as follows (the duration of studies being eight semesters in all):

Courses

Students enrol in the following departments: acting, stage and radio producing, film and television direction, playwriting, and production management. A camera department was established in 1970, and a department of film editing in 1971. The acting, playwriting and production management departments are common to all sections (that is, for theatre, film, radio, and television). Students decide which section they will finally adopt at the time of taking their final examinations.

Admission

By secondary-school certificate and competitive examination.

Syllabus

Acting. Common to all sections: dramatic art, diction, voice training, stage movement, acrobatics, fencing, acting styles, world drama and theatre, Yugoslav drama and theatre, film history, psychology, elements of social science, foreign language, paramilitary training, degree task in major subject. Required studies: music, mime, singing, dance. Film and television exercises. Practical acting in theatre, cinema, radio or television after the fourth semester.

Film and television production. Film and television direction, film and television script-writing, techniques of film production, film editing, diction, music, styles, film theory, film history, psychology, elements of social science, foreign language, paramilitary training, degree task in major subject. Required studies: cinema and television camera; television techniques; film analysis. Exercises: film production, television production, film production techniques. Practicals: work as an assistant producer or producer of a film or television production after the fourth semester.

Camera. Camera art and techniques; the art of photography, film and television production; film editing; elements of physics and chemistry; sensitometry; film direction techniques; film theory; history of the camera; the figurative arts; art history; acrobatics; elements of social science; foreign language; paramilitary training; degree task in major subject. Required studies:

set design, make-up, sound techniques, television camera, costuming, special effects. Exercises: work as a cameraman in all of the exercises for prospective directors in the second, third and fourth years. Practicals: after the first year, a two-month apprenticeship in the film laboratory. After the second year, two months assisting in or shooting a professional film. After the sixth semester, assisting in or shooting in a television studio.

Playwriting. Common to all sections: film and television scenarios, theatrical staging and radio production, cinema and television direction, aesthetics, world drama and theatre, drama and theatre in Yugoslavia, film theory, film history, elements of social science, foreign language, paramilitary training, degree task in major subject. Required studies and exercises: scriptwriting, film scenarios. Practicals: work in professional theatre, cinema, television or radio, after the fourth semester.

Production management. Common to all sections: economic and legal aspects; show organization, organization of film production, organization of radio and television activities, staging, technical production of film, music, world drama and theatre, drama and theatre in Yugoslavia, film history, film styles, elements of social science, foreign language, paramilitary training, degree task in major subject. Required studies: radio techniques, television techniques, distribution and presentation of films, cultural politics in the communes. Practicals: work in the professional theatre, cinema, radio, or television after the fourth semester (must be done before starting degree task).

Film-editing. Film and television editing, film direction and television production, film production techniques, camera, photography, film history, film theory, the figurative arts, music (counterpoint and form), scenario, diction, psychology, elements of social science, foreign language, paramilitary training. Required courses: sound techniques. Practicals: participation in films shot by students for television.

Teaching staff

Apart from university professors, the academy depends largely on people in Yugoslav cultural and artistic life, including some of the leading film-makers.

A certain freshness was brought to film-making by some of the academy's recent graduates whose talent has attracted attention and won awards at national and international festivals.

Ljubljana and Zagreb theatre academies

The theatre academies at Ljubljana and Zagreb are university institutions which also teach film and are organized on the same lines as the Belgrade Academy.

The academy at Ljubljana has existed for quite some time, but offers comparatively little film teaching, as the country served is so small. The Zagreb academy has only recently started film courses.

In 1964, the Film Institute in Belgrade opened a film school for students from developing countries which lasted until 1967.

Teaching was in French, and took two semesters. Finance was provided under the Yugoslav technical assistance programme. The primary subject was documentary but students also studied aesthetics and world film (through many film screenings). The theory course was based on teaching at the Film Education Centre, and the practical side received particular attention as most of the students were being introduced to film for the first time. The main problem was selecting candidates, which was done in their own countries without the film school having any say in the matter.

In certain cases, although the course time was short and most candidates did not satisfy the admission conditions, the results were quite appreciable.

It may be suggested at this point that experiences on the lines of those in Yugoslavia can serve as a point of departure for a discussion on the education of film-makers in developing countries which lack a great film-making tradition.

The terms of the problem in such situations are somewhat paradoxical: should we train people who can then start film-making, or start producing films and the process will incidentally look after the training also? Import foreign film-makers, or await the return of our own after their education in countries where film-making is advanced? This problem remains unresolved in many countries, and is very complex, since countries can create their own cinema only with the aid of their own key film people.

Yugoslav cinema has now attained wide recognition abroad (awards at international festivals, more films exported, and so on). This was made possible by raising general and professional education standards at all specialization levels. But the really decisive element was having time enough to allow talent to mature and reveal itself.

This does not happen overnight, especially in a national cinema that is only starting, for magic formulas simply do not exist. The best (not very feasible) solution would seem to be to promote film-making and educate the key personnel simultaneously. Education via production can be provided in the Grierson way by getting the most talented young journalists, writers, painters, musicians, teachers together and allowing them, with the help of a few technicians, to express themselves in short films of different kinds, while at the same time having them follow film and television courses under home and foreign film experts. This is one possible teaching basis for a new national cinema.

The future

The film education issue can be reduced to certain specific, practical problems: (a) improving and adapting the curricula of certain existing film schools and exchanging information on this subject; (b) enabling young film-makers to get in touch with and be absorbed into professional film production; and (c) the very important one of finding the kind of teaching programme best suited for countries which are only just starting to make their own films.

If we accept the apparently incontrovertible idea that mankind is in the midst of a vast technical revolution in audio-visual techniques, we can also confidently say that we are on the threshold of an image-dominated civilization. It is in any case evident today that the insatiable demand for images must lead to a boom in film and television production of many different kinds and hence, a boom in the demand for key personnel in cinema and television.

Our present 'image civilization' depends on film and television (and various inventions such as video cassette, transmission by satellite, mural-screen television, and so on). But film and television are really quite separate and only occasionally touch and overlap.

First of all, there is the element of time: film-making is separated from film-showing, whereas in television (considered, of course, as a means of expression) making and presentation are simultaneous. In practice this means that the same event (a football match, for example) can have a television life and a film life. Its television life is the direct transmission. The director operates in real time and the viewer participates directly in the game (or in landing on the moon). Everything is arranged as a direct representation where the actors think of the spectators, and even communicate with them.

The film life of this game, however, depends on the director and the editing (real time no longer applies). The spec-

The opening session of the Unesco Meeting
on the Education of the Film-maker
for Tomorrow's Cinema held in Belgrade being filmed
for Yugoslav television.
[Photo: Institute Za Film, Belgrade.]

tator next day sees an artistic transposition of the event which, regardless of whether it is accurate or not, constitutes a documentary or reporting film. However, the videotape presentation of the entire game more or less simulates direct participation using a simple 'photocopy'—but the television audience never regards it as such. Film rather than television is involved, since editing necessarily takes place as the different videotape parts are fitted together. A complete recording on videotape of an event may be available in the relatively short time necessary for its transposition; it may serve as a photographic record of the event; there is also the similar case of filmed theatre. In any of these cases there is a transition between the event and the film of it that confirms the existence of a structural difference between film and television. The fact that such transitions exist in the case of most broadcasts is irrelevant to the argument.

This point has been emphasized in order to show that much present-day television is film rather than television—a difference that should be reflected in the training provided. Television as it is today is in great need of film creators. Tomorrow, when many more stations begin to televise directly and television really becomes 'a window on the world', there will be a great need for those who can create in television language.

Things being as they are, it is perhaps no accident that it is so difficult to say what education for television should be. Graduate students employed in television do not always realize that they are really working in film. On the other hand, those who have specialized in film sometimes feel they are betraying film by working for television in order to make a living.

Naturally, things are not always so clear-cut in the practical world and, even if 80 to 90 per cent of present television is really film, how are these filmed programmes to be financed and what kinds of people are needed to produce them, once we admit that film language is more complex than simple magnetic recording?

It is not the plan to go into these questions in detail, but so far as the theses advanced here are valid, they could have the following implications.

First, film production for cinema showing is now only one of the possible forms and probably no longer the most important; in view of the development of other forms (television programmes, for example) it will probably stagnate as regards quantity (but not, on the contrary, as regards quality). Film schools (but not necessarily their teaching programmes) are adequate in this respect, and probably can cope.

Second, the daily increasing need for television programmes (usually involving film) demands that measures be taken now to educate key creative staff—primarily for film. This means that we must think now about attracting a relatively large number of people into existing or new arrangements for providing film education.

Third, new film recording techniques, and the potentially enormous increase in places where films can be shown thanks to videocassettes and so on, should lead to an increase of still undefined dimensions in film production of all kinds. The corollary is a corresponding increase in education facilities to accommodate the people who will produce these films.

Fourth, these increases raise a major cultural problem. Experience so far indicates that the increase in quantity is obtained at the expense of quality—in almost inverse proportions as the number of hours of television broadcasting increase. This could be very negative in cultural terms so far as these particular mass media are concerned.

We do not believe that there is any analogy with radio stations, which were able (at least in Yugoslavia) to increase quality at the same time as they increased hours of broadcasting. They have inexhaustible sources (tape and disc recordings). Could we make enough film recordings to satify the potentially enormous future demands? On the creative side their production is more expensive than music, novels, newspapers, direct television broadcasts or their photocopies. Videocassettes will undoubtedly open a new market, and attract enormous capital resources to the production of films for all kinds of purposes. But who is to actually produce this material?

Fifth, in this complex process we can see what will be demanded of film education in the future, greater than anything we can now imagine. It will be still some time before the programmes and personnel shortage that we can foresee becomes really critical. We can suppose that the existing forms of filmmaking education will no longer be sufficient. One day, probably, great sections of the population will become apprenticed at all educational levels, from primary school to schools specializing in various aspects of film-making and television education, or even to the level of scientific research.

For these reasons we feel that the thinking and research should start now regarding preparations for future developments in cinema and television and the educational arrangements they will demand. Meanwhile we should make a determined effort to induce schools at all levels to take up the question of including film and television in their curricula; to get existing film schools to extend their range and get new ones of various kinds opened; and, finally, to ensure the training of those who will be responsible for the education on a vastly increased scale of key personnel for film and television.

Appendix

Unesco Meeting on the Education of the Film-maker for Tomorrow's Cinema, Belgrade, Yugoslavia (22-26 May 1972)

Participants

Satish Bahadur (India), *Professor of Film Appreciation, Film and Television Institute of India, Ministry of Information and Broadcasting, Poona.*

Ola Balogun (Nigeria), *University of Ife, Institute of African Studies, Ife-Ife.*

Youssef Chahine (Egypt), *Film Director, Cairo.*

Manuel González Casanova (Mexico), *Director, University Centre of Cinematographic Studies, Universidad Nacional Autonoma.*

Momćilo Ilić (Yugoslavia), *Director, Institut Za Film, Belgrade.*

Bertil Lauritzen (Sweden), *Director, Dramatiska Institutet, Filmhuset Borgvägen, Stockholm.*

Keith Lucas (United Kingdom), *Director of the British Film Institute.*

Raymond Ravar (Belgium), *Director, International Institute of the Dramatic Arts and Mass Media (INSAS), Ministry of Education, Brussels.*

Paulo Emílio Salles Gomes (Brazil), *Film director and professor of cinematography at the University of São Paulo.*

Léopold Schlossberg (France), *President Director General, Institute of Higher Education in Cinematography, Paris.*

George Stevens Jr (United States), *Director, The American Film Institute, Washington D.C. and California.*

Naosuke Togawa (Japan), *Dean, College of Arts, Nihon University, Tokyo.*

V. Zdan (U.S.S.R.), *Vice-Rector, State Film Institute (VGIK).*

Observers

Félix Mariassy, *International Liaison Centre for Cinema and Television Schools (CILECT).*

Robert W. Wagner, *University Film Association.*

Unesco Secretariat

d'Arcy Hayman, *Head, Arts Education Section.*